Strategic Management

Christian Managerial Concepts

KWAKU AHENKORA

TIMELESS EDUCATION

Business and Management
Executive Editor: Prof. Isaac Ferguson
Editor: D. Henry
Print and Production: Charleston, SC, USA
Marketing: Concept Consulting

First published in Great Britain 2003

Credits and acknowledgements borrowed from other sources
and reproduced appear on appropriate pages within text.

Copyright © 2013 Timeless Touch
Chigwell, IG7 4WA

The right of Kwaku Ahenkora to be identified as author has been
asserted by him in accordance with the Copyright, Designs and Patents
Acts, 1988.

ISBN: 978-0954571535

Timeless Education is an imprint of Timeless Touch

In loving memory of Isaac and Mercy

Kwaku Ahenkora, BSc. Mphil. (Kwame Nkrumah University of Science and Technology), MBA (University of Liverpool), PhD (Trinity College Newburgh/ Canterbury Christchurch University) is a strategy consultant and lecturer with a broad range of sector, industry and international experience. He has published articles in management journals on the strategic management of both business and social enterprise organisations, including Christian organisations. He is a member of the Chartered Management Institute (UK) and Head of Department for Marketing, Logistics and Corporate Strategy at Christian Service University College.

CONTENTS

Acknowledgments

I acknowledge the contributions of Christian strategic managers who have shared their perspectives with me. I thank Peter Brierley who directed me to his work in the field. I appreciate the advice and contributions of Dr Robert Kennedy. The final thanks go to Salome and Samuel for their love and support.

1

Introduction

Over the last fifty years strategic management has gone through a series of evolutionary changes and has become established as a legitimate field of research and managerial practice. It is widely recognised that the effective leadership and management of today's organisations require good strategic thinking and management.[1] Strategic management can be understood in terms of the processes by which the organisation, in a dynamic and, above all, interactive manner, seeks to ensure that it responds to its general environment.[2] To cope with change in today's competitive world, strategic managers must address the three interrelated tasks of managing strategy, managing the organisation and practicing strategic management.[3]

Managing strategy in the marketplace involves designing, executing, and refining strategies that win in a changing marketplace. Strategy is the means which the organisation creates, and leverages change in and around the marketplace, to provide superior value (compared with that of rivals) for customers. Next, managers are required to manage by continually reconfiguring the organisation – how it thinks, how it operates. Without such internal change, the organisation can't hone its capacity to identify, adapt to, and leverage environmental change. Lastly, managers must practice strategic management by continually enhancing the linkages or interface between strategy and the organisation. Traditionally, strategic management research and practice- crafting and executing strategy- have enabled business organisations to compete effectively and succeed in the marketplace.[4]

Until recently, however, strategic management concepts were used in the business domain and were not part of the public and social sector vocabulary. Today, perhaps more than ever before, public and social sector organisations, including religious organisations, are using private sector strategic management methods.[5] Strategic management in the social sector is at the rudimentary stage; it is still emerging as an area for academic inquiry, yet strategic management concepts developed primarily for private business purposes are now an expectation for the social sector. But should they become one-size fits-all prescription?

Purpose

Strategic management tools and concepts are aimed at addressing the fundamental question in the field of strategic management: how do firms achieve and sustain competitive advantage?[6] The competitive strategies of religious organisations are attempts to address this question[7]. Religious organisations are social enterprises that create, maintain, and exchange supernaturally-based general compensators.[8] There are common and differentiating features between commercial and social entrepreneurship[9], and subsequently, the use of strategic management concepts in the different enterprise contexts.

This book provides perspectives on how the distinctive nature and central role of mission in Christian organisations create multifaceted value propositions and conceptions different from those of business organisations. It focuses on two questions. First, why do managers of Christian organisations use strategic management concepts? Second, how does the nature of the organisation affect the use of strategic management concepts? It is intended to engage students of strategic management/ planning, academics and practitioners with the discourse and academic interest in the strategic management of social enterprises and Christian organisations.

In addressing the questions raised, the book provides the UK Christian managerial viewpoint and highlights the need that managers of Christian organisations operating in a competitive environment have for using strategic management concepts (Chapter 2). This is followed by an outline of the application of strategic management concepts to religious organisations, focusing on the Christian organisation (Chapter 3). Using practitioner perspectives on strategic purpose and value creation, strategic thinking and planning (Chapter 40), the book explores   emergent Christian concepts (Chapter 5) and provides opportunities for further elaboration on these concepts (Chapter 6).

This book provides perspectives on how the distinctive nature and central role of mission in Christian organisations create multifaceted value propositions and conceptions different from those of business organisations.

NOTES

[1] Peter F. Drucker, *Managing the nonprofit organisation* (New York: HarperCollins Publishers, 1992), 59.

[2] Jonathan Sutherland and Dianne Canwell, *Key Concepts in Strategic Management* (New York: Palgrave-McMillan, 2004),258.

[3] Laim Fahey and Robert M. Randall, "Managing Marketplace Strategy," in *The Portable MBA in Strategy*, eds. Laim Fahey and Robert M. Randall (New York: John Wiley & Sons, 2001), 8.

[4] See Kwaku Ahenkora and Ofosuhene Peasah. Crafting strategy that measures up. *International Journal of Business and Management* 6, 2011:278

[5] Kevin P. Kearns, *Private Sector Strategies for Social Sector Success: the guide to strategy and planning for public and nonprofit organisa tions* (San Francisco: Jossey-Bass Inc., 2000), xiii

[6] See David J.Teece, Gary Pisano and Amy Shuen, "Dynamic capabilities and strategic management. *Strategic Management Journal*,Vol 18:7, 509-533.

[7] Kent D. Miller, "Competitive Strategies of Religious Organisations," *Strategic Management Journal* 23, 2002:436

[8] Rodney Stark and WS Bainbridge *A Theory of Religion* (New York: Peter Lang, 1987), 42.

[9] James Austin, Howard Stevenson and Jane Wei-Skillern, 'Social and Commercial Entrepreneurship: Same, Different, or Both?" *Entrepreneurship Theory and Practice*, 30, 2006:2

2

The Christian Managerial Case

As organisations serve purpose and use tremendous amount of time, effort, investments, assets and resources, it makes perfect sense to manage, measure, monitor and maximise value. A good strategy is expected to deliver value, usually economic value (or the net present value of the future cash flows from a strategy).[1] However, given the need for strategic thinking in the current hypercompetitive environments, there is the greater need to re-evaluate the assumptions of traditional static strategy models.[2]

More importantly, strategic management is not short of prescriptions and directives with regard to successful strategic recipes and it is imperative that we look at its one-size fits-all prescriptions for private, public and social sector organisations. The problem many managers face when they attempt to develop and implement a more strategic approach is that the majority of the best-known and most widely used strategy tools are increasingly being seen as out of date. For example, tools such as the growth share matrix, Porters five forces and three generic strategies were all developed against the background of a very different environment and sector from the one within which many managers operate today, and as a consequence have a number of limitations.

Strategy perspectives

In the evolution of strategic management, a diversity of partly competitive and partly supplementary perspectives have emerged. Attempts have been made to classify these perspectives into classical strategy perspectives, modern strategy perspectives and post-modern strategy perspectives.[3] Historically, an organisation's strategy has been thought of as an integrated plan. The most frequently cited definitions of organisation strategy emphasised concepts such as goals, resource allocation, and especially plans.[4] These concepts form the essential elements of the classical perspective of strategic management corresponding to what several authors also refer to as planning, rational, rational comprehensive or synoptic approach.

In these classical strategic management theories, strategy is considered as a deliberate planning process (formal), initiated by top management (top-down), based on an elaborate industry analysis (rational) and aimed at designing a cohesive grand strategy for the organisation (consistency). The classical perspective still pervades the literature on strategic management and created the foundation of the strategy field. It informed scholarship and practice; when strategy became a capstone course in most curricula of business schools; when large enterprises created strategic planning departments, and strategy consultants developed various tools and techniques (e.g.,SWOT analysis, BCG matrix, GE business screen, Mckinsey's 7S model).

The classical strategic management perspectives also added some strategic dogmas to the field. For instance, the classical management perspective still works on the assumption that the CEO can design an explicit 'grand strategy' for the entire enterprise.[5] However, it has been shown that strategies are not always explicitly formulated, but can emerge spontaneously without *a priori* intentions, from the bottom-up initiatives of frontline managers and in turbulent environments planning is often insufficient and leads to rigidity.[6]

As researchers and practitioners found untenable some of the normative assumptions of the classical perspective, modern strategic management perspectives gained influence in the discipline. In these perspectives, strategy is depicted as a messy, disorderly, and disjointed process around which competing factors contend.[7] Modern strategy perspectives posit that strategy making is an incremental process of 'muddling through' that is distinct from the linear rational perspective, since different subunits display a disorderly proliferation of preference orderings and divergent views of cause-effect relations.

Some questions still remain about the nature of incrementalism within the modern strategic management perspectives as, apparently, strategic options and resources are not a sufficient basis for adaptation. Adaptation requires participants to be able to make sense of their environment and know what to adapt to. Reality is defined through a process of social interchange in which perceptions are affirmed, modified, or replaced according to their apparent congruence with the perceptions of others.[8]

Strategy in the post-modern perspective has been defined as strategic schema or frames of reference that allow the organisation and its environment to be understood by organisational stakeholders.[9] In this regard, the key managerial question is how to develop adequate strategic schemas that enable the firm to create or adapt to competitive change. Strategic management in this approach, therefore, involves creating and maintaining systems of shared meaning that facilitate organised action.

From a post-modern perspective, the Christian managerial interest is best served by the development of contextual social enterprise strategic management framework.

> *From a post-modern perspective, the*
> *Christian managerial interest is best served*
> *by the development of contextual social*
> *enterprise strategic management framework*

Strategy and competitive advantage

Today's managers face increasing levels of change while also coping with increased complexity and, frequently, reduced levels of resources. Strategic management, therefore, has become an expectation, not only on the part of the company but also the individual manager. Strategy is the direction and scope of an organisation over the long term[10]. Corporate history shows that high-performing enterprises often initiate and lead, not just react and defend and they are always the product of astute, proactive management, rather than the result of lucky breaks or a long run of good fortune.[11]

An organisation with a well-articulated strategy can achieve sustained competitive advantage over those organisations that lack strategic vision.[12] Strategic thinking provides a cognitive map that supplies the underlying logic for combining, deploying, and activating resources within the organisation and among the firm's strategic business units.[13] Through this process, it focuses and channels organisational competencies toward effective accomplishment of goals. Strategy must, therefore, be crafted with competitive advantage as the basis.[14]

The implications of a poorly developed and poorly implemented approach to thinking and planning has led to some writers suggesting that many companies have lost the art of strategy-making; few managers put strategy as their starting point in building their company and very few put strategy at the top of their list of priorities.[15] Insofar as it is possible to identify the characteristics of those organisations in which managers have not lost sight of the significance of planning and strategy, they are that :

- There is a clear sense of purpose and direction
- Strategies are clearly articulated
- There is continuous investment in people, products and markets
- Resources and effort are clearly focused upon those elements that are seen to be important and that give or contribute to competitive advantage
- There is commitment to the long term
- The management team is determined to overcome obstacles and roadblocks

- There is an emphasis upon implementation
- Management are concerned with creating their own future, rather than having it created for them by others.

Churches in the United Kingdom that achieve their missions for growth have clear strategic visions and create strategy to move towards their goals.[16] Leaders of such churches are known to think widely, spanning past, present and future and are able to explain where their church is going and how to get there.[17]

> *Churches that achieve their missions for growth have clear strategic visions and create strategy to move towards their goals*

Strategic adaptive change

Change creates choices and strategy reflects managerial choices among alternatives and signals organisational commitment to particular products, markets, competitive approaches and ways of operating the organisation. The choices organisations make depend to a large extent on their understanding of current and potential change and their capacity to anticipate, create and leverage change in scope (i.e. choice of products and customers), posture (how aggressive it competes in its chosen business) and goals (the choice of what attainment it pursues).[18] Today, strategy has to be adapted to real-life relationships between people (employees, customers, suppliers and so forth), gradually introduced and crafted and re-crafted as circumstances change and the validity of the underlying assumptions is tested, proved or disapproved.[19]

The use of strategic management concepts and terms are currently becoming a norm in the UK Christian organisational context. Managers of local churches are expected to manage strategically[20], and the competitive business analogy has been applied to Christian organisations in the United Kingdom.[21]

Strategy in context

The various perspectives in strategic management show the plurality of concepts, theories and approaches in the field. These perspectives indicate that strategy and strategic management exist in particular contexts and provide the impetus for expanding the knowledge base in pluralistic fashion. An attempt to develop a single paradigm consisting of universal concepts and laws covering the entire strategic management field is apt to be misleading. Strategy context is concerned with the circumstances within which strategy process operates and strategic content is developed. The focus of strategy context is on the 'when, where and why' of strategy.

The strategy process addresses issues such as how is and should, strategy be made, analysed, dreamt-up, formulated, implemented, changed and controlled.[22] It also focuses on the actions that lead to and support strategy, and relates to issues concerning the generation and implementation of strategy or how an organisation, through either intentional or unintentional actions, arrives at its strategic position. [23]

There are two schools of thought on the role of context in strategy.[24] One view is that context influences (perhaps even determines) both strategic process and content providing the boundaries for strategic activity and limitations on strategic direction and strategic dynamism. An alternative view suggests that strategists and strategic activity create the strategic context. Relevant contextual issues centre on the manager and managerial action, organisational context and industry context. For nonprofit organisations such as charities, churches, private schools and foundations, the mission, underlying values and ideology are significant in shaping strategy development.[25] The fundamental purpose of the Christian organisation is a unique contextual characteristic that shapes strategy.

The value of strategic thinking is usually defined in terms of economic value or the net present value of the future cash flows from a strategy. Both organisational and economic factors are determinants of firm performance. For businesses, shareholder value in the stock market tends to be the ultimate output measure of a company's performance.[26] Value creation, however, is not only financial for social enterprises.[27] For UK Christian organisations, the value of strategic thinking lies in its contribution to church growth in the UK.

> *For nonprofit organisations such as charities and churches, the mission, underlying values and ideology are significant in strategy development.*

Notes

[1] Tony Grundy and Laura Brown, *Be Your Own Strategy Consultant: Demystifying Strategic Thinking* (London: Thomson Learning,2002),155.

[2] Gary Hamel, *Leading the revolution* (Boston, MA: Harvard Business School Press, 2000), 10

[3] Henk W. Vorbeda, "Crisis in Strategy," *European Management Review* 1, 2000:36.

[4] See for example, K.R. Andrews, *The Concept of Corporate Strategy*, (Homewood II: Dow Jones-Irwin, 1971),7.

[5] Henk W. Vorbeda, "Crisis in Strategy," *European Management Review* 1, 2000:36

[6] Henry Mintzberg and JA Walters. "Of strategies, deliberate and emergent. *Strategic Management Journal*, 6, 2003:257-272

[7] See for example J.B Quinn, "Managing strategic change", *Sloan Management Review*, 21, 1980:3-20.

[8] Henk W. Vorbeda, "Crisis in Strategy," *European Management Review* 1, 2000: 37

[9] Combatoire K. Prahalad and Gary Hamel, "The core competence of the organisation", *Harvard Business Review*, 68, 1990: 85

[10] Gerry Johnson and Kevin Scholes, *Exploring Corporate Strategy* (London: FT Prentice Hall, 1999), 60

[11] Arthur A. Thompson and A.J. (Lonnie) Strickland, *Crafting and Executing Strategy* (New York: McGraw-Hill, 2001), 28.

[12] Coimbatore Krishnarao Prahalad and Gary Hamel, *The Core Competence of the Corporation*, Harvard Business Review, 1990:79-91

[13] Coimbatore Krishnarao Prahalad and Richard Bettis, "The dominant logic: new linkage between diversity and performance," *Strategic Management Journal*, 7, 1986:485-501.

[14] Michael E. Porter, "The State of Strategic Thinking", *The Economist* , May 23,1987

[15] Michael de Kare Silver, *Strategy in Crisis* (Basingstoke: Macmillan Press,1997),12.

[16] Robert Gills, *A Vision for Growth* (London: SPCK, 1994), 2.

[17] Peter Brierley, *Leadership, Vision and Growing Churches* (London:Christian Research, 2003), 23.

[18] Laim Fahey and Robert M. Randall, "Managing Marketplace Strategy," in *The Portable MBA in Strategy*, eds. Laim Fahey and Robert M. Randall (New York: John Wiley & Sons, 2001), 8.

[19] Robert Koch *The Financial Times guide to Strategy: how to create and deliver a useful strategy* (London: Prentice Hall, 2000),5.

[20] Peter Brierley, *Leadership, Vision and Growing Churches* (London:Christian

Research, 2003), 23.

[21] Andrew Sentence, *Successful Leadership in a Competitive Environment* (London: Christian Research,2003),14.

[22] B. DeWit and R. Meyer, Strategy: Process, content, context: An International perspective (London: Thomson Learning, 2004), 5

[23] Huff, AS. & Reger. R.K. (1987) "A review of strategic process research". *Journal of Management*. 13, 1987:217 (211-236)

[24] B. DeWit and R. Meyer, Strategy: Process, content, context: An international perspective (London: Thomson Learning, 2004), 10

[25] Gerry Johnson and Kevin Scholes, *Exploring Corporate Strategy* (London: FT Prentice Hall, 1999), 34.

[26] Tom Copeland, Tim Koller and Jack Murrin (McKinsey and Company , Inc.) *Valuation: Measuring the Value of Companies* (New York:John Wiley, 2000), 3.

[27] Tony Grundy and Laura Brown, *Be Your Own Strategy Consultant: Demystifying Strategic Thinking* (London: Thomson Learning,2002), 227.

3

Strategic management and religious organisations

The previous chapter has shown the general expectation that managers and leaders of churches operating in post-modern hyper competitive environments, should manage strategically. This chapter extends the thought further and considers the application of strategic management concepts to religious organisations and the Christian enterprise. It is useful to begin with a brief overview of the history of strategy.

History of strategy

It is generally stated that the roots of strategy go back to Alfred Sloan's re-organisation of General Motors in 1921 and its documentation published forty years later in 1963. However, it was Peter Drucker who set the Strategy ball rolling with his 1946 book, Concepts of the Corporation when he studied General Motors, IBM and Sears Roebuck, and concluded that the most successful companies were centralised and good at goal-setting. He was also the first to promote the idea that the purpose of a business was external, that is, in creating and satisfying customer needs.

The study of Strategy and the development of the micro-economic foundations of strategic thinking, is also traced to Alfred Chandler who was active and influential from the late 1950s. In 1962, he wrote the book, *Strategy* and *Structure* in which he proposed that corporations should develop their strategy before deciding their structures.[1] He defined strategy as the setting of long-term goals and objectives, the determination of courses of action, and the allocation of resources to achieve objectives.

In 1960 Theodore Levitt published Marketing Myopia in the Harvard Business Review, one of the first attempts to look at corporate strategy from a radical and broad perspective.[2] In 1965, Igor Ansoff produced the monumental book *Corporate Strategy*, which provided a detailed blueprint for planning a firm's objectives, expansion plan, product-market positions and resource allocation. Another important development in Strategy was the establishment of the management consulting firm, Boston Consulting Group (BCG) in 1964 by Bruce Henderson. The company developed two powerful tools in strategy, the 'Experience Curve' and the 'Growth/ Share Matrix. The management consulting firm extensively used market analysis and research together with financial theory to produce the microeconomic analysis of competitors and their relative costs.

The most important books in the 1970's were *The Nature of Managerial Work* (1973) by Henry Mintzberg, and *Strategic Management* (1979) by H. Igor Ansoff. The 1980s saw the emergence of the writers, Michael Porter and Kenichi Ohmae. Porter, the Harvard Academic, became prominent in the Strategy field with his very important 1980 book, *Competitive Advantage: Techniques for Analysing Industries and Competitors*. He argued in this book that the profitability of corporations was determined not only by a firm's relative competitive position but also by the structural characteristics of the firm's industry, which could be described in clear, micro-economic terms. Kenichi Ohmae described brilliantly how Japanese companies had benefited by using Strategy (though without Strategy Consultants or Western Academics). In his 1982 book, *The Mind of the Strategist: The Art of Japanese Business*, he showed how Strategy is most effective when it combines analysis, intuition and willpower in the pursuit of global dominance.

Notable contributors to strategic thinking during late 80s and early 90s period included Gary Hamel, C.K. Prahalad, John Kay; the trio of management writers from the UK Ashridge Strategic Management Centre, Andrew Campbell, Michael Goold and Marcus Alexander. In 1989, Gary Hamel and C.K. Prahalad wrote a ground-breaking article entitled *Strategic Intent*. They argued that successful companies had ambitions out of all proportion to their positions and had a commitment to change the rules of the game. The authors followed this with another influential article, *The Core Competence of the Corporation*, in which they argued that the real key to strategy was a firm's distinctive skills, technologies and assets, and its collective learning ability. This extended the 'resource-based' view of strategy. In 1994, Andrew Campbell, Michael Goold and Marcus Alexander wrote the book *Corporate-level Strategy* and argued that the corporate centre should be seen as 'parent' and develop 'parenting skills' to help it operating companies, and that unless the centre comprised the best possible parent for each business, they should be divested.

Changes in strategic thinking

Strategic management research is littered with a diversity of perspectives. In the early years, strategic thinking and planning constantly evolved as it was alternatively embraced and rejected by leading organisations in the United States and Europe.[3] The one cardinal management sin that spans national and industry boundaries has been the persistent belief that there is a single formula for corporate success, coupled with rapid shifts in conviction as to what exactly that formula might be.[4] Through periods of diversification or divestiture, growth or recession, regulation or deregulation, the best and brightest academicians and management consultants convinced corporate management to adopt a succession of strategic theories or processes, each vaunted as a single formula for success. Over the years, scores of these management concepts such as benchmarking, customer segmentation, value chain analysis, scenario planning, reengineering, quality management were adopted as the answer to the strategy problem of the moment.

In the 1960s and 1970s, strategic planning enjoyed widespread, almost unqualified, acceptance. The emphasis then was on the creation of a new staff function, the development of elaborate planning processes and procedures, all supported by an array of new analysis, techniques and methodologies such as the experience curve, the growth/ share matrix, and PIMS (profit impact of market share). The fatal flaw in this approach was that staff took over the strategy-making function from the managers; in time, the process, with its elaborate methodologies and documentation, came to dominate the staff, yet little or nothing changed operationally.

Faced with implementation problems during the recessions of 1980 and 1982, many companies abandoned the planning process, shifting the power back to managers. Without a strategic framework for their planning, line managers fell back on familiar habit, making tactical decisions based on short-term factors. In the late 80s, when strategic planning was still under a cloud, it was pointed out that there were no substitutes for strategic thinking.[5] The mid-to late-1980s saw a hesitant return to strategic planning, renamed strategic management. The proponents simplified the process, streamlined documentation, and placed the main responsibility for strategy development and execution in the hands of management teams at the corporate or business unit level. However, strategic planning was skewed toward the needs of financial approach (mergers and acquisition and financial deal-making) which was then the dominant themes of the period.

The 1990s was characterised by well-hyped approaches to strategic success including total quality management (TQM), core competencies (or capabilities), and most notably, reengineering. Reengineering attracted management attention with its implied promise of combining strategic restructuring with the tactical benefits of cost reduction. However, reengineering was abandoned in midstream as there was an underestimation of the human factor in redesigning processes. The quest for one-size fits-all solution seemed to have led executives into a blind alley. Suspicion persists that executive understanding and support for strategic planning is fragile and will last only until the 'next big thing' comes along. Sustained commitment, however, comes only from a radical re-perceiving of the true nature and role of strategy, for the greatest benefit of strategic planning is that it encourages managers to consider and take action on multiple fronts, moving from one strategic issue to another.

The economic and resource views of strategic thinking

Historically, the dominant thinking in the strategy discipline throughout much of the 1970s and 1980s was the Industrial Organisation (IO) economic concept that is most associated with the work of Porter. The strategic planning in the IO school of strategy was concerned with industry structure, as it was the major determinant of profitability. Thus, many strategic planning methods consisted of analysing industry forces to determine the attractiveness of an industry and how to influence the structure of the industry and ultimately, profits.

Strategic thinking based on such industry analysis is not an adequate means for formulating strategy in a dynamic environment.[6] Preparing an in-depth, system-wide analysis of the competitive environment, and then implementing a strategy based on that analysis, assumes that the environment is not changing in crucial respects more quickly than one can develop and implement the strategy. But few, if any, industries are exempt from discontinuity today. Traditional IO strategic thinking assumes that industry trends can be reliably extrapolated, and this supposition is also the basis for many strategic analysis tools, including competitor analysis, strategic groups, Profit Impact of Market Share (PIMS), and diversification typologies such as the classification of business units into dogs, stars, cash cows. Because the increasing rate of change has put pressure on firms to react more quickly, time is often seen as a source of competitive advantage.

The rapid-paced digital operating environment requires all observers of today's Internet Age to address one cosmic question: How can we compete in unpredictable, chaotic times?[7] Current thinking includes hyper-competition, disruptive technologies, strategy as revolution, strategy as real options, competing on the edge and surfing the edge of chaos. The common theme in today's thinking seems to be on how to reinvent the organisation, expect the unexpected, and compete when the future is not certain or forecastable.

An alternative view to the economic view is the resource-based view of strategy. This perspective suggests that the fundamental source of competitive advantage lies not in industry structure, but instead, in a firms internal resources. The firm's special capabilities and competencies are the principal drivers of firm profitability and strategic advantage.[8] Resources are said to confer competitive advantage to the extent that resources must be difficult to create, buy, substitute, or imitate. There is a shift of focus on tangible assets as the sole source of advantage to intangible assets, which include knowledge, core competencies, learning and 'invisible assets' such as brand image or corporate culture. The logic underlying many of these ideas involves 'the collective learning in the organisation, especially with how to coordinate diverse production skills and integrate multiple streams of technology. The focus on intangible assets has had ripple effects in managerial practice. There has been a greater emphasis on knowledge management as organisations seek to harness and leverage their intellectual assets. Moreover, the reality that the key strategic advantage of many firms is primarily knowledge-based has become important.

Defining Strategy

Over the last 50 years or so, a considerable amount has been written about strategy and from this a variety of definitions and strategic perspectives have emerged. However, one of the first to discuss strategy in a structured way was the Chinese General Sun Tzu[9], who, in his book *The Art of War*, suggested that it was better to overcome one's enemies by wisdom rather than by force alone: 'One should appraise a war first of all in terms of five fundamental factors and make comparisons of various conditions of the antagonistic sides in order to assess the outcome. The first of the fundamental factors is politics; the second, weather, the third, terrain; the fourth, the commander; and the fifth, doctrine.' Sun Tzu's book is one of the oldest military treaties yet discovered and addresses the interrelationships and interpersonal relationships primarily concerned with diplomacy. However, much has been learnt from the book in terms of strategy and has been used as an important source for strategic management.

Early attempts described strategy as the answer to two fundamental questions: What is our business, and what should it be? Following on from this, strategy was described as the determination of the basic long-term goals and objectives of an enterprise and the adoption of courses of action and the allocation of resources necessary for carrying out these goals. More recently it is suggested that strategy is a pattern of objectives, purposes or goals and major policies and plans for achieving these goals, stated in such a way as to define what business the company is in or is to be in and what kind of company it is or is to be. While there exists arguments against giving a definition of strategy, for the reason that all too often such definitions lead to overly long discussions about the semantics, strategy is the direction and scope of an organisation over the long term: ideally, one which matches its resources to its changing environment and in particular its markets, customers or clients so as to meet stakeholder expectations.[10]

The above perspectives position strategy as a deliberate set of actions, but a more organic approach is also necessary. There is a strong tendency to slip into talking about it as a response that the organisation makes to an environment. This depersonalises the game and strategy is understood in mechanical terms, where one thing moves in predetermined ways in relation to another thing. The inevitable result is the lack of insight into the real complexities of strategic management because in reality organisations and their environments are not things, one adapting to other but groupings of people interacting one with another.[11]

Henry Mintzberg has proposed that strategy is concerned with five Ps and that there are eight different types of strategy. The five Ps of strategy are:

- Planning, which deals with the direction of the organisation
- Ploys, which are designed to deal with and outwit the competition
- Patterns, which represent a logical stream of actions
- Position, which relates to how the organisation is located in the market place
- Perspectives, which reflect the management team's view of the world.

Mintzberg's eight different types of strategy are as follows:

- Planned strategies, which represent a series of deliberate and precise intentions
- Entrepreneurial strategies, which emerge as the result of a personal vision
- Ideological strategies, which reflect the collective vision of the management team
- Process strategies, which result from leadership controlling the process
- Umbrella strategies, which emerge from a set of broad objectives set by the leadership
- Disconnected strategies, as the result of sub-units being only loosely connected
- Consensus strategies, where members converge on patterns

- Imposed strategies, where the external environment or a parent company dictates patterns of action

Strategy and planning

Irrespective of the type of strategy that an organisation adopts, the extent to which a strategy is achieved is determined to a large extent by the ways in which organisational resources are managed; something that is achieved through business and marketing planning process.[12] This is based on the following reasons:

- Organisations must plan to coordinate their activities
- Organisations must plan to ensure the future is taken into account
- Organisations must plan to be rational
- Organisations must plant to control.

However, there are practical problems with planning and they include:

- How best to identify and manage organisational stakeholders
- How to anticipate long(er)-term futures and develop the most appropriate product or market portfolio in order to leverage competitiveness
- How to plan for things that might foreseeably go wrong with mainstream plans
- How to manage products and turn marketing dreams into reality
- How to seek out major cost-cutting and contribution-creating opportunities and make the required changes to enhance productivity
- How to create a base for innovation and then to harness the ability of the enterprise to change effectively its products, services and processes
- How to make the most of unexpected opportunities and respond positively to shock events.

Strategic plan is, therefore, an overarching series of activities which aim to implement and develop a new concept, deal with a problem, or establish the foundation of the business's objectives in the coming period.[13] Strategic planning is a continual process, with the monitoring and control procedures providing the information for the development of this and future strategic plans.

Schools of strategic thinking

To aid current thinking on strategy and how strategic thinking perspectives have developed, it has been suggested that:

'We are all like the blind man and the strategy process is our elephant. Everyone has seized some part of the animal and ignored the rest. Consultants have generally gone for the tusks, while academics have preferred to take photo safaris, reducing the animal into two dimensions. As a consequence, managers have been encouraged to embrace one narrow perspective or another- like the glories of planning or the wonders of core competencies. Unfortunately, the process will only work for them when they deal with the entire beast as a living organism.' [14]

Mintzberg has summarised and identified 10 views of the strategy process and how they have developed.

The Design School

In the opinion of the design school, proposed by Selznick, strategy development focuses very largely upon matching internal strengths and weaknesses with external opportunities and threats. Clear and simple strategies are developed by senior managers as the result of detailed and conscious thought and are then communicated to others further down the organisational hierarchy

The Planning School

The key advocate of the planning school is Ansoff. In many ways similar to the design school, the planning school is based on a series of formal and distinct steps characterised by checklists and frameworks. Highly cerebral and formal in its nature, it is typically driven by staff planners rather than senior managers as the key players

The Positioning School

Based firmly upon the work of writers such as Michael Porter, the school emerged from earlier work on strategic positioning by organisations such as the Boston Consulting Group and the PIMS researchers, and reflects thinking on military strategy and ideas of Sun Tzu. Strategy is reduced to a series of formal analyses of industry situations. Planning is seen to be highly analytical process, with emphasis being placed upon hard data. Among the framework to have emerged from the school are strategic groups, value chains, and game theories.

The Entrepreneurial School

The entrepreneurial school, advocated by Schumpeter, gives emphasis to the role of the chief executive and strategies are based not so much upon detailed designs, plans, positions and framework, but upon visions of the future and the organisation's place within this. A key element of the school is the argument that all organisations need a visionary leader.

The Cognitive School

The cognitive school is concerned not so much with the type or nature of strategy as with the mental processes that underpin any strategy that emerges. Proposed by March and Simon, the areas of particular emphasis have proved to be cognitive biases and aspects of information processing.

The Learning School

The proponents of the learning school are Cyert, March, Hamel and Prahalad. With its origins in the ideas of incrementalism (a series of small steps rather than any large one), venturing and emergent strategy (strategy grows from a series of individual decisions rather than as the result of a tightly defined process), strategy development is seen to take place at levels within the organisation. There is an emphasis upon retrospective sense-making ('we act in order to think as much as we think in order to act') and a belief that strategy formulation and implementation are linked.

The Power School

The power school proposed by Allinson and Pfeiffer and others, is seen by many to be a relatively minor school. The power school gives emphasis to the idea that strategy making stems from power. This power can be seen both at a micro-level in that strategy emerges as a result of politicking between organisational actors, and at a macro-level in terms of external alliances, joint ventures and network relations.

The Cultural School

Whereas the power school concentrates on self-interest and fragamentation, the cultural school of Rhenman and Normann, is based on a common interest, with strategy development being seen as a social process rooted in the organisational culture. One of the most influential forces in the thinking in this area proved to be the impact of Japanese management in the 1970s and the 1980s, as it became evident that difficult-to-copy cultural factors could contribute to competitive advantage.

The Environmental School

The advocates of the environmental school are Hannan and Freeman and Pugh. Whereas much thinking on strategy rests upon how the organisation uses its degrees of freedom to develop strategy, the environmental school focuses upon the significance and implications of demands placed upon the organisation by the environment. Included within this is 'contingency thinking', in which consideration is given to the responses expected of the organisation as the result of specific environmental conditions, and 'population ecology', which argues that there are significant constraints upon strategic choice.

The Configuration School

Seen by many to be a more extensive and integrative school of thought than those referred to above, this is characterised both by the view that the organisation is a configuration of coherent clusters of characteristics and behaviours, and by the belief that change must be seen as a dramatic transformation. The key proponents of the configuration school are Chandler, Mintzberg, Miles and Snow.

Strategy formulation

There are four principal or generic approaches to strategy formulation, namely, the classical approach, the evolutionary approach, the processual approach and the systematic approach. [15]

The Classical Approach

The advocates of the classical approach to strategy formulation are Ansoff, Sloan and Porter. The essential underpinning is economic theory, with its advocates arguing that profit maximisation is an important objective and that the strategist's task is to position the organisation or business unit in such a way that this can be achieved. Rigorous intellectual analysis represents an essential input into the process, and is designed to contribute to the organisation achieving a degree of control over the internal and external environment.

The Evolutionary Approach

Similar in a number of ways to the classical school of thought, strategy evolutionists such as Henderson (of the Boston Consulting Group), Friedman and Peters, differ in that they believe that because the strategist cannot control the environment, the idea of a single strategy route is inappropriate. Instead, they argue, the planner needs to recognise the options open to the organisation and keep these options open for as long as possible. Its advocates also argue that because large organisations are inherently slow and inflexible, the notion of an all-embracing strategy is unrealistic. In turn, this leads to a belief that long-term strategies can often be counterproductive and that higher levels of long-term performance can often be achieved by a sense of fast-moving, short-term cost reduction processes. However, in a competitive market place the organisation should launch as many small initiatives as possible and see what works; the competitive processes inherent in the market place should then allow the best initiatives to flourish and an overall strategy should begin to emerge as a pattern from the market place, in this way the market dictates the strategy, not the manager. [16]

The Processual Approach

This pattern of thought, advocated by Mintzberg[17] and Hamel, emerged from the evolutionary school, and is based on the idea that a worthwhile strategy can only emerge as the result of the strategists detailed involvement in the day-to-day activities of the business. The environment is too powerful and unpredictable for the strategist to overcome or manage it purely on the basis of intellectual analysis and that- unlike the evolutionists- markets are not sufficiently or inherently efficient to allow for performance maximisation. Organisations represent a collection or coalition of individuals and interests, goals- and strategy- emerge as the result of a bargaining process. Planning and implementation must be firmly interlinked or else central corporate planning departments lose their value. Mintzberg in particular believes that effective strategy involves a series of small steps that then coalesce into a pattern, and that the key to higher performance is an emergent rather than a deliberate strategy. This view is also based firmly upon the idea that in the absence of the right competencies, strategy and plans are to all intents meaningless.

The Systemic approach

This approach is strongly promulgated by Whittington and Morgan. This reflects a belief that there is no one strategy model that is applicable to all types of organisation, but that both the objectives and the strategy process are the result of the strategist's social and cultural backgrounds and of the social context in which they are operating. This view gives emphasis to the way in which strategy and the strategy process are not necessarily objective and rational but, particularly in multinational organisations, are a reflection of an amalgam of possibly very different forces that have their origins in social systems. The most obvious ways in which these differences are manifested within multinationals include attitudes to profit, risk, levels of accountability, group versus individual decision-making, timescales and indeed the notion of the free market. Advocates of the systemic school argue that a focus upon implementation is essential and that this is significantly influenced by organisational sociology.

Prescriptive and Emergent Strategies

Attempts to simplify the plethora of approaches to strategy formulation have led to categorising the process of corporate strategy development into two distinct frameworks: prescriptive and emergent strategies.[18]

Prescriptive strategy process

A prescriptive strategy is one where the objective has been defined in advance and the main elements have been developed before the strategy commences. In studies of prescriptive strategy, close parallels have been drawn with what happens in military strategy- for example, as seen in the early Chinese military historical writings of Sun Tzu; the writings of the nineteen-century German strategist, Clausewitz, and those of Captain B H Liddell Hart who wrote about the First World War. All these have been quoted by corporate strategists. Prescriptive business strategy is sometimes seen as being similar to sending the troops (employees) into battle (against competitors) with a clear plan (the prescriptive strategic plan) that has been drawn up by the generals (directors) to be implemented.

Prescriptive strategy analysis has its basis in economic theory. Adam Smith, writing in the eighteenth century, took the view that human beings were basically capable of rational decisions that would be motivated most strongly by maximising their profits in any situation. Moreover, individuals were capable of making rational choice between options, especially where this involved taking a long-term view. Adam Smith has been quoted with approval by modern strategists, economists and politicians. Modern strategy theorists, such as Michael Porter, have translated profit maximisation and competitive warfare concepts into strategy techniques and structure that have contributed to prescriptive strategy practice. Porter suggested that what really matters is sustainable competitive advantage over competitors in the market place: only by this means can a company have a successful strategy. Strategists such as Ansoff and Andrews follow in the long line of those writing about strategic planning systems who employ many of these concepts.

While there are some advantages with the prescriptive approach, Mintzberg researched decision making at corporate level and suggested that prescriptive strategy approach is based on a number of dangerous assumptions as to how organisations operate in practice. Six major assumptions of the prescriptive process that may be wholly or partially false include:

- The future can be predicted accurately enough to make rational discussion and choice. However, as soon as the government or competitor does something unexpected, the whole process may be invalidated.

- It is possible and better to forgo the short-term benefit in order to obtain long term good.

- The strategies proposed are, in practice, logical and capable of being managed in the way proposed. Given the political realities of many organisations, there may be many difficulties in practice.

- The chief executive has the knowledge and power to choose between options. He/ she does not need to persuade anyone, nor compromise on his/her decisions. This may be extraordinary naïve in many organisations where the culture and leadership seek discussion as a matter of normal practice.

- After careful analysis, strategy decisions can be clearly specified, summarised and presented; they do not require further development, nor do they need to be altered because circumstances outside the company have changed. This point may have some validity but is always not valid.

- Implementation is a separate and distinctive phase that only comes after a strategy has been agreed. This is extraordinary simplistic in many complex strategic decisions.

Emergent Strategies

Despite the advantages claimed for a prescriptive strategy system operating at the centre of organisations, there is significant research to show that some of the assumptions were incorrect. Theories of emergent strategy have developed, as an alternative view of the strategy process. Emergent corporate strategy is a strategy whose final objective is unclear and whose elements are developed during the course of its life, as the strategy proceeds.[19] In the light of the observation that human beings are not always the rational and logical creatures assumed by prescriptive strategy,[20] various commentators have rejected the dispassionate, long-term perspective approach. They argue that strategy emerges, adapting to human needs and continue to develop over time. Given this, they argue that there can be only limited meaningful prescriptive strategies and limited value from long-term planning.

Research into how companies and managers develop corporate strategy in practice has shown that the assumption that strategies are always logical and rational does not take into account the reality of managerial decision making. Examples are summarised below. [21]

- Managers can handle only a limited number of options at any one time-this is referred to as 'bounded rationality'
- Managers are biased in their interpretation of data. All data is interpreted through our perceptions of reality.
- Managers are likely to seek a satisfactory solution rather than maximise the objectives of the organisation. In other words the profit-maximising assumption of economic theory may oversimplify the real world.
- Organisations consist of coalitions of people who form power blocs. Decisions and debate rely on negotiations and compromise between these groups, termed 'political bargaining'. Researchers found that the notion of strategy being decided by a separate, central main board does not accord with reality.
- To take decisions managers rely on a company's culture, politics and routines, rather than on a rational process of analysis and choice. (Who you know and how you present your strategic decision is just as important as the content of the strategy.)

The development of corporate strategy is more complex than the prescriptive strategies imply; the people, politics and culture and organisations all need to be taken into account. [22,23] These perspectives view corporate strategy as a process whereby the organisation's strategy is derived as a result of trial, repeated experimentation and small steps forward: in this sense corporate strategy is emergent rather than planned. The implications for corporate strategy based on the emergent view include:

- Strategies emerge from confused background and often in a muddled and disorganised way: the resulting strategies themselves may therefore be unclear and not fully resolved.

- The prescriptive strategic process is unlikely to reflect reality: options identified will not be comprehensive and the selection process will be flawed.
- Considering 'implementation' after the rest of the strategy process does not reflect what usually happens.
- Managers are unlikely to seek the optimal solution: it may not be capable of identification and, in addition, may not be in their personal interests.
- Working within an organisation's routines and culture will allow the optimal culture to emerge rather than be forced by an artificial planning process.

The advantages of emergent strategy process are that it accords with actual practice in many organisations, especially with regard to people issues like motivation. It takes into account the leadership, culture and politics of an organisation. In addition, it also allows strategies to experiment and develop as strategic circumstances change, delivering flexibility during the process.

However those who favour prescriptive strategic approaches have a number of basic concerns about emergent strategy[24]:

- It is entirely unrealistic to expect board members at corporate level simply to sit back and let operating companies potter along as they wish. The headquarters consists of experienced managers who have a unified vision of where they wish the group to progress. It may take several steps to arrive at this vision, but the group should make visible progress rather than just muddling along.
- Resources of the group need to be allocated between the demands of competing operating companies; this can only be undertaken at the centre. It therefore demands some central strategic overview.
- It is entirely correct that there are political groups and individuals that need to be persuaded that a strategy is optimal, but to elevate this process to the level of corporate strategy is to abdicate responsibility for the final decision that needs to be taken.
- In some industries where long time frames are involved, decisions have to be taken and adhered to or the organisation would become completely muddled.

- Although the process of strategy selection and choice has to be tempered by what managers are prepared to accept, this does not make it wrong; rational decision making based on evidence has a greater likelihood of success than hunch and personal whim. Thus debate should take place but be conditioned by evidence and logic.
- Management control will be simpler and clearer where the basis of the actions to be undertaken has been planned in advance.

A summary of the approaches to strategy formulation narrows down to a balanced perspective: organisations often pursue what may be called umbrella strategies; the broad outlines are deliberate while the details are allowed to emerge within them.[25] Thus the emergent strategies are not necessarily bad and deliberate ones good, effective strategies mix these characteristics in ways that reflect the conditions at hand, the ability to predict as well as the need to react to unexpected events.

> *Organisations often pursue umbrella strategies; the broad outlines are deliberate while the details are allowed to emerge within them.*

Levels of strategic management

There are three essential elements to strategic management[26]:

- Awarenes: understanding the strategic situation
- Formulation: choosing suitable strategies
- Implementation: making the chosen strategies happen

Strategy formulation, therefore, needs to ensure that any planned course of action is consistent with the general strategy of the business and with the business's ability to achieve these objectives. Normally, strategy formulation takes place at three different levels of an organisation[27]:

- Corporate level- where strategy formulation is based on objectives and strategies for achieving these objectives
- Business level- which is often known as competitive strategy formulation, and deals with strategy formulation in relation to every area in which the organisation is involved
- Functional level- which is strategy formulation related directly to ensuring that either corporate level or business level strategy can be achieved through manipulation of current functional activities.

Strategy Context

This section on strategy context takes a look at the general organisational context, information on profit strategies and the strategic management context for nonprofit organisations.

The Organisational Context

The external environment of organisations is literally the big wide world in which both public- and private-sector organisations operate. Whatever the nature of their business, organisations do not and cannot exist in splendid isolation from the other organisations or individuals around them, be they customers, employees or suppliers. The term 'environment' is more appropriately interpreted as the external context in which organisations find themselves undertaking their activities. Each organisation has a unique external environment that has unique impacts on the organisation, due to the fact that organisations are located in different places and are involved in different business activities, with different products, services, customers and so on.[28]

The benefits of analysing the external environment include the following:

- Managers in the organisation achieve a greater understanding and appreciation of the external environment leading to improvement in long-term strategic planning
- Highlighting of the principal external environmental influences generating change;
- Anticipation of threats and opportunities within a timescale of long enough duration to allow responses to be considered. Economic environment, tax policies, employment levels, technological advances, and social movements such as those

involving labor, religion and politics are examples of specific contextual factors.[29]

Profit strategies

At the business level strategy is concerned with competing for customers, generating value from the resources and the underlying principle of the sustainable competitive advantages of those resources over rival companies. Strategy can be seen as the linking process between the management of the organisation's internal resources and the economic and social environment in which it exists.[30]

Strategic management principles have been historically developed almost exclusively from a business perspective- for example, competitive advantage, customer-driven strategy and corporate governance. For many writers, purpose is explored or defined solely in terms of business organisations, with profit featuring somewhere in its definition.[31]

Nonprofit strategies

Although the definitions of nonprofit organisations is very broad, it covers charitable, voluntary and public interest bodies that are not owned by the state. Nonprofit organisations raise their income from a variety of private, voluntary and variable sources. For many nonprofit organisations, the mission of the organisation may also need to remind the stakeholders of the inspiration that originally led to the foundation of the organisation- in the case of volunteer organisations in particular, this may be what will drive them forward.

Today, perhaps more than ever before, public and nonprofit organisations use strategic management methods to help them survive in a volatile and competitive environment. Nonprofit organisations of all types have launched entrepreneurial commercial ventures and are aggressively using fees for service to augment charitable donations and government grants.[32] Nonprofit hospitals and other health care organisations are using strategies of horizontal and vertical integration in order to gain greater control and stability in their turbulent history. Today if one works in nonprofit organisations, one may use a vocabulary that was once heard only in the executive suites of private corporations.[33] One would be looking for *market niches* that capitalizes on the organisation's *comparative advantages*. Maybe one is worried about *competitive threats* in the *marketplace* and how to provide *customers* with *value-added* products and services. One may be using management techniques like *portfolio analysis* or *breakeven analysis* and tracking financial indicators like *profit margins* and *liquidity ratios*.

Attempts have been made to apply the concept of competitive strategy to public and nonprofit organisations. [34] However, there has also been backlash, primarily among scholars, against business-oriented philosophy in government. Critics make the appropriate observation that government agencies and nonprofit organisations are not businesses and should not be operated as such. What nonprofit organisations need is an approach to strategic management that incorporates their unique circumstances.

> *What nonprofit organisations need is an approach to strategic management that incorporates their unique circumstances.*

The religious economy

The use of established research in sociology and economics has helped to bring theoretical strategic management perspective to the study of religious organisations.[35] Achieving competitive advantage is of great concern to the field of strategic management.[36] In applying strategic management theory to religious organisations, it is important to find the distinguishing features of religious organisations and to establish the analogy to competitive firms.

There are useful definitions to clarify religion and the products of religious organisations. Religion is defined   as systems of general compensators based on supernatural assumptions.[37] Religious organisations, therefore, are social enterprises whose primary purpose is to create, maintain and exchange supernaturally-based general compensators bundled with rewards.[38] Rewards are anything humans will incur costs to obtain and compensators are postulations of reward according to explanations that are not readily susceptible to unambiguous evaluation. With regards to rewards, the boundaries between religion and other industries can be blurry. Blurring occurs through secularisation of religious organisations, and through 'spiritualisation' of secular organisation. However, supernatural compensators are distinct products of religious organisations for which there are no direct secular substitutes.

> *Religious organisations are social enterprises whose primary purpose is to create, maintain and exchange supernaturally-based general compensators and rewards*

Examples of rewards are as follows:
- *Church membership*: which confers status and legitimate standing in the community, and which makes it possible to secure other religious rewards
- *Attendance at worship services*: which in addition to any specific religious meanings are also social occasions, and provide whatever rewards obtain from such
- *Participation*: in religious organisations and activities, including such disparate things as the choir, the men's fellowship, or the singles club

- *Child socialisation*: conveying a cultural and moral heritage to children as well as supplying rewards such as membership in scouting and sporting groups.

The list of compensators includes the following:
- *Religious doctrines*: which promise to make the burdens of this life bearable, to make guidance and help available, and to offer reparations for earthly suffering in the life after death
- *Religious experiences*: a release of pent-up emotions and a source of confidence in the authenticity of compensators, such as when a person has a vision or speaks in unknown tongues
- *Prayer and private devotionalism*: mechanisms for seeking divine aid and guidance, for confessing guilt, for gaining comfort
- *Particularism or moral superiority*: reassurance that no matter how little one seems to matter in this world of affairs, one is among those chosen by God and possesses an elite religious identity.

Standard strategic management analysis distinguishes suppliers, buyers, and the internal production process of the firm.[39] The separation of value chain activities and corresponding stakeholders is often less appropriate for religious organisations than for firms in other industries. The technology of religious organisation is known to involve collective action and this blurs the distinctions among stakeholders: consumers are simultaneously suppliers and producers. In this regard religious organisations exhibit a rare combination in the nonprofit sector: mutual benefit activities supported by voluntary contributions.[40]

Religious competition

A critical observation has been made that regardless of the origin and nature of their beliefs, the survival and growth of religious organisations depend on access to resources from the external environment; and this is the fundamental challenge shared by all organisations.[41] The material aspects of religious organisations have been often prominent and always inescapable. Resources of interest include physical and financial assets, number of adherents and their levels of time commitment and effort. Rivalry among religious organisations is overt- as among proselytising organisations- or takes the more subtle form of simply trying to retain and generate higher commitment among existing adherents. Rivalry among religious organisations can be intense, particularly in unregulated religious markets.[42] This competition takes place within a dynamic social context characterised by modernisation, globalisation, pluralism, privatisation, and changing gender roles.

The rivalry among religious organisations is described in the following statement[43]:

'..the religious tradition, which previously could be authoritatively imposed, now has to be marketed. It must be 'sold' to a clientele that is no longer constrained to 'buy'. The pluralistic situation is, above all, a market situation. In it, the religious institutions become marketing agencies and the religious traditions become consumer commodities. And at any rate a good deal of religious activity in this situation comes to be dominated by the logic of market economies.'[44]

Sustainable competitive advantage

Recent developments in strategic management and organisation theory show the complementarity of institutional and economics-based models of competitive advantage. Three conditions underlie the competitive advantages of religious organisations.[45] First, credible commitment and social perceptions of legitimacy are highlighted as key determinants of the success of religious start-ups. Second, the sources of inimitability identified in the resource-based view of the firm provide insights into sustainable advantage. Third, strictness is the basis of market segmentation and product positioning.

The products of religious organisations are credence goods- credence qualities are those, which although worthwhile, cannot be evaluated in normal use.[46] Since religious rewards and compensators are intangibles, the key to marketing religion is to create the perception of credibility. Credible commitments by suppliers foster confidence, not because they prove the validity of religious claims but because they signal suppliers' convictions.[47] Indicators of religious commitment include:

- A minimal professional staff whose financial compensation is low and independent of customer contributions/payments
- Heavy reliance on part-time and volunteer workers (and thus reliance on payments of time and service rather than money)

- A congregational structure, which limits the need for full-time professionals and provides a source of credible product endorsements

The intangible nature of religious services heightens causal ambiguity. Attributing competitive advantage to supernatural causes indicates to would-be imitators that the basis for success is inherently ambiguous.[48]It is recognised that because the technology of religious organisations is collective and interpersonal it is infused with social complexity. Copyrighted materials, such as music or literature, can provide the basis for auxiliary business units within religious organisations.[49]

Market segmentation

The distinction between rewards and compensators in religion offers other opportunities for price discrimination. The availability of secular substitutes for religious rewards makes premium-pricing untenable. Accommodating churches, for example, must compete with other clubs and entertainment providers in the market for rewards. On the other hand compensators have few rewards.

Shaping Industry Structure

At the organisational level, religious organisations have individual approaches to gaining and sustaining competitive advantage. Additionally, religious organisations have the potential to influence the environments in which they compete. The strategic management perspective of industry dynamics is that an organisation by itself or in coordination with other industry players can make strategic moves to reshape the nature of competition. Two aspects of strategic moves within industry are political strategies and alliances. Government policy toward religious organisations is a critical determinant of relative competitive positions and the resources available to the sector as a whole; government policy toward religion ranges from subsidisation to suppression.[50]

Strategic thinking and UK Christian organisations

In the UK there are increasing attempts to highlight strategic management insights into the leadership and management of Christian organisations, especially churches. A comprehensive research conducted with 38,000 UK churches concluded that if churches are to pursue their purpose, strategic thinking must be at the forefront.[51] Another study looked at a wide range of aspects of church life which might relate to growth and also included a Belbin leadership-style profile of the minister, thus enabling the type of leader to be statistically correlated with growth or decline for the first time across a substantial number of churches. [52] Of all the various natural gifts that leaders may have there was only one associated more with fast growing than declining churches- the Shaper. This Shaper type of leader is known by:

- His/her ability to think widely, spanning past, present and future
- Their capacity to think laterally, and often 'outside the box'
- She/he asks 'What do we have to do to stay in business?' (where business means 'retaining a sense of identity and purpose for the institution')
- Being able to explain where their church is going, and to do so in a few crisp words
- Having a clear strategy of how to get there

Looking at the situation the Church faces in modern society, the competitive analogy is quite appropriate and the sources of competition are the encroachment of work and leisure activities into the traditional day for church activities, the increasing lure of secular activities and the growth of alternative religions. The church, however, is not a business, and so leaders should be cautious in the way they apply these competitive concepts in the church context. [53]

> *The church is not a business and so leaders should be cautious in the way they apply competitive concepts in the church context*

This is true in business where people are paid for what they do and it is even pertinent in church life that relies on voluntary effort from committed and dedicated supporters. Hence any programme of change must have the buy-in and support of the congregation or fellowship or it will fail.

Contextualisation

Bosch provided the theological and historical background on contextualisation within Christianity.[54] The contextualisation process involves reaffirming traditional beliefs while continuously adapting their expression to environmental conditions. If a religious organisation lacks a competitive advantage in the provision of compensators, it will eventually shed this product line and focus on rewards, or exit entirely. A Christian organisation that fails to establish sustainable advantages in the provision of supernaturally-based compensators divests these lines. If it has profitable set of rewards, it continues to operate as a secular business. The historical experiences of religious-affiliated Christian colleges and universities provide examples of such secularisation.

A Christian organisation that fails to establish sustainable advantages in the provision of supernaturally-based compensators divests these lines. If it has profitable set of rewards, it continues to operate as a secular business. The historical experiences of religious-affiliated Christian colleges and universities provide examples of such secularisation.

40

Value Creation

Historical developments

The historical development of value is known to have its roots prior to the industrial revolution.[55] Before the industrial revolution, companies were relatively small and their internal complexity was low. Also the external environment of companies was relatively stable and clear. Value creation was relatively straightforward, simple and obvious. In the 18th and 19th Century, production processes and systems were aimed at promoting and evaluating the efficiency and production of decentralised production processes and not yet on measuring and managing value creation as such.

However, at the end of the 19th Century, Alfred Marshall saw profit as the residual income accruing to a firm's owner, a return to the investment of his own capital and to the pains he suffers in exercising his 'business power' in planning, supervision and control. Frederick Taylor and Harrington Emerson later developed Scientific Management (using detailed physical manufacturing standards), enabling a simple translation to financial standards. Corporations became more complex because they now had a diversified product assortment and often had several types of company activities instead of just one. Allocation of assets over the various activities and, as a result, better information on these activities became more important. Management Accounting introduced Return on Investment (ROI), at first only at top management level for allocating resources and judging performance.

In 1983, Grant made references to using time value of money for deciding about investment project. In 1954 Dean published an article in the HBR about using Discounted Cash Flow (DCF) practically for valuing investment proposals and other decisions. Later, methods were introduced such as residual income, responsibility accounting and transfer pricing. In 1964, Sharpe introduced the Capital Asset Pricing Model (CAPM) and in 1973 Black and Scholes introduced their formula for calculating the value of financial options.

In 1964 Peter Drucker wrote 'Managing for Results' and in 1986, Alfred Rappaport wrote his ground-breaking book, 'Creating Shareholder Value'. In 1994 Jim McTaggart used the term 'value based management' in his book 'The Value Imperative: Managing for Superior

Shareholder Returns. From now on, thinking in financial/shareholder value terms was firmly rooted in business and corporate strategy. MVA, TSR, EVA and CFROI were developed in order to determine the value of corporations and investments. The world of Corporate finance was also rapidly professionalising, leading to increased attention for managing value in Mergers and Acquisitions. Leveraged buy-outs became very popular in the 1980s, as public debt markets grew rapidly and opened up to borrowers that would not previously have been able to raise loans worth millions of dollars to pursue what was often an unwilling target. This presented a major stimulus for managers that ran their companies in ways that mainly served their own private interests (improved authority, control and compensation), often at the expense of the companies' owners, shareholders, and long-term strength to change their behaviour.

From the 1980s Activity Based Costing (ABC) and similar concepts (Activity Based Management, Transaction-Based Costing) were developed, enabling more precise and more future-oriented measurement of profitability and economic value by products, channels, markets, processes and organisations. Risk management methods such as RAROC (1970) became more popular in the nineties, combining risk management and economic profit valuation for allocating capital and financial institutions. Following the birth of the World Wide Web (WWW) in 1994, many new strategic information/ knowledge related opportunities and technologies arose, simultaneously increasing the complexity of the internal and external environment of corporations. A spectacular value increase of intellectual capital in corporations was the consequence. New intangible asset valuation models arrived.

Change management also gained ground during this period as a way to deal with increasing discomfort levels in ever faster changing companies. In 1998 Luehrman transferred the formula for determining the value of options into dealing with uncertainty over time in strategic decision making. Real Options, Scenario Planning and Game Theory were also developed to deal with strategic complexity and agility.

In 1992 Kaplan and Norton published the Balanced Scorecard model which became popular, enabling organisations to translate a company's vision and strategy into implementation, working from both the financial perspective as well as the customer, business process, learning and growth perspectives.[56] Several new technologies such as Business Performance Management, Business Intelligence and Business Simulation were developed to support complex decision making and management processes in corporations.

At the beginning of the third millennium, with the apparent Internet bubble burst, the Enron Accounting crisis in 2001 and several other corporate scandals throughout the world, accountants, stock analysts, top management, business schools, media, shareholders and investors were all blamed. Among the most prominent ideas to prevent further disasters proposed for the future included attention for stakeholders' interests and a long term view towards value creation. This resulted in interest in holistic value based management in organisations. The financial crisis of 2008 emphasised the urgent need for this approach.

Value propositions

Due to the influence of business corporations on society, many people with different backgrounds have discussed the corporate purpose they should serve. In countries with market economy it is generally agreed that companies should pursue economic profitability. But organisations also have certain social responsibilities.[57] There has always been, and continues to be, vigorous debate on the importance of shareholder value relative to other measures such as employment, social responsibility, and the environment. The debate is often cast in terms of shareholder versus stakeholder.

Value based management is the management approach that ensures corporations are run consistently on value (normally, maximising shareholder value) and it includes the following[58]:

- Creating value (ways to actually increase or generate maximum future value- strategy)
- Managing for value (governance, change management, organisational culture, communication, leadership), and
- Measuring value (valuation)

Shareholder Value Perspective

The shareholder value perspective emphasises profitability over responsibility and sees organisations primarily as instruments of its owners. An organisation's success can be measured by things such as share price, dividends and economic profit, and see stakeholder management rather as a means than as an end in itself. Social responsibility is not a matter for organisations but society is best served by organisations pursuing self-interest and economic efficiency. The purpose of the company is, first and foremost, to maximise the shareholder value, within what is legally permissible. At least in ideology and legal frameworks, the United States and the United Kingdom have given the most weight to the idea that shareholders are the owners of the corporation, the board of directors is their representative and elected by them, and the objective function of the corporation is to maximise shareholder value.[59]

Managers focus on value creation for two reasons. First, in most developed countries, shareholder influence already dominates the agenda of top management. Second, it is posited that shareholder-oriented economies appear to perform better than other economic systems and other stakeholders do not suffer at the hands of shareholders.

Stakeholder value perspective

The stakeholder values perspective emphasises responsibility over profitability and sees organisations primarily as coalitions to serve all parties involved. Stakeholder value advocates believe an organisations success should be measured by the satisfaction among all stakeholders and see stakeholder management both as an end and a means. They believe social responsibility is an organisational matter and claim society is best served by pursuing joint-interests and economic symbiosis. Recognising the moral claims by stakeholders other than the shareholders introduces other values than financial value in the spectrum of what needs to be pursued by the organisation. Stakeholder management is normative to creating shareholder value. The view is that nurturing high levels of trust with all parties within and outside the organisation and pursuing the joint interests of all stakeholders is not only more just, but will also maximise societal health.

Measuring value

Financial measures of performance have evolved, and today the concept of economic value added (EVA) is prevalent. The core ideas around value creation and measurement are that in the real market, you create value by earning a return on your invested capital greater than the opportunity cost of capital. The more you can invest at returns above the cost of capital the more value you create (i.e, growth creates more value as long as the return on capital exceeds the cost of capital). Towards this end one selects strategies that maximise the present value of expected cash flows or economic profit. The value of a company's shares in the stock market equals the intrinsic value based on the market's expectations of future performance, but the market expectations of future performance may not be an unbiased estimate of performance. Also the returns that shareholders earn depend primarily on changes in expectations more than actual performance.[60]

Value creation in today's companies is increasingly represented in the intangible drivers like innovation, people, ideas, and brand.[61] Increasingly, efforts are being made to identify the specific intangibles that are perceived to drive value for a given industry. Non-financial value drivers vary by industry. As social enterprises borrow strategic management concepts, there is the need to understand the specific intangibles that are perceived to drive value in these organisations.

Summary

This chapter has provided information on the historical perspectives on strategic management and the application of concepts to religious organisations. The history of strategy and strategic management shows its military roots, its application by business organisations that have predominantly been the focus and the current adoption of key concepts of strategic management by religious organisations. Several authors have made significant contributions to the field.

Strategic management still remains a paradigmatic field, and in its evolution it has spawned off diversity of perspectives. The strategy process has been equated to the blind touching the elephant, and each person's description fits with their own perceptions. Traditional strategic thinking assumes that industry trends can be reliably extrapolated, and this supposition became the basis for many strategic analysis tools. An alternative view to the economic view is the resource-based view of strategy. Attempts have been made in the literature to clarify the definitions of strategy, strategic management, strategic thinking and strategic planning. The terms seem to be used interchangeably in the literature but mention has been made of the inherent practical differences. .

> *As social enterprises borrow strategic management concepts, there is the need to understand the specific intangibles that are perceived to drive value*

Several schools of strategic thinking exist in the strategy process. However, attempts to simplify the plethora of approaches to strategy formulation have led to categorising the process of corporate strategy development into two distinct frameworks, prescriptive and emergent strategies. A prescriptive strategy is one where the objective has been defined in advance and the main elements have been developed before the strategy commences. Emergent corporate strategy is a strategy whose final objective is unclear and whose elements are developed during the course of its life, as the strategy proceeds. There are three elements to the strategy process: analysis, formulation and implementation. Strategy is formulated at the functional, business or corporate levels of the organisation.

The concept of competitive strategy has been applied to public and nonprofit organisations where the strategic context is broader than the commercial enterprise. Nonprofit organisations, therefore, need an approach to strategic management that borrows the relevant concept from the business sector. Established research in sociology and economies were used to bring theoretical strategic management perspective to the study of religious organisations

Religious organisations are social enterprises whose primary purpose is to create, maintain and exchange supernaturally-based general compensators. Blurring occurs through secularisation of religious organisations, and through 'spiritualisation' of secular organisation. However, supernatural compensators are distinct products of religious organisations for which there are no direct secular substitutes. Recent developments in strategic management and organisation theory show the complementarity of institutional and economics-based models of competitive advantage. Religious rewards and compensators are intangibles. In the UK, there are increasing attempts to highlight strategic management insights into the leadership and management of Christian organisations.

The historical developments of value creation show financial measurement as the predominant focus and value of the business organisation. In recent years, however, due to corporate scandals, there is renewed interest in intangible measures of corporate value and for organisations to take a long-term view towards value creation. Propositions have been made to ensure that corporations are run consistently on value, maximising shareholder or stakeholder value.

The strategies of religious organisations are dynamic responses to conflicting pressures for traditionality and innovation. These pressures result from cultural change within and outside the organisation, and rivalry among existing and new religious organisations. Also, looking at the role Christian organisations play in modern society, the competitive analogy is quite appropriate. Contextualisation, however, requires continual innovation that maintains core beliefs. The products of religious organisations, supernatural compensators and rewards, are intangibles and there are increasing efforts to identify the specific intangibles that drive value for a given industry.

> *Contextualisation requires continual innovation that maintains core beliefs*

Notes

[1] Alfred Chander, *Strategy and Structure*, (Cambridge, Mass: MIT Press, 1962),

[2] Theodore Levitt, "Marketing Myopia", *Harvard Business Review*, 38 (4), 1960: 45-56

[3] Ian Wilson, "There is no Universal Strategy Formula," in *The Portable MBA in Strategy*, eds. Laim Fahey and Robert M. Randall (New York: John Wiley & Sons, 2001), 385.

[4] Ian Wilson, "There is no Universal Strategy Formula," in *The Portable MBA in Strategy*, eds. Laim Fahey and Robert M. Randall (New York: John Wiley & Sons, 2001), 387.

[5] Michael E. Porter, "The State of Strategic Thinking", *The Economist* , May 23,1987

[6] Richard Bettis and M.A.Hitt "The New Competitive Landscape", *Strategic Management Journal,* 16, 1995:7-19

[7] Jeffrey L. Sampler, "Digital Strategy," in *The Portable MBA in Strategy*, eds. Laim Fahey and Robert M. Randall (New York: John Wiley & Sons, 2001), 132.

[8] Coimbatore Krishnarao Prahalad and Gary Hamel, *The Core Competence of the Corporation*, Harvard Business Review, 1990:79-91

[9] Sun Tzu, The Art of War, New York: Harper Collins, 1994.

[10] Gerry Johnson and Kevin Scholes. *Exploring Corporate Strategy* (London: FT Prentice Hall, 1999),82.

[11] See for example, RD Stacey, *Strategic management and organisational dynamics,* (London: Pitman, 1993), 21.

[12] Giligan and Wilson: pg 46

[13] Jonathan Sunderland and Dianne Canwell, *Key Concepts in Strategic Management.* (Basingstoke : Palgrave Mcmillan, 2004),261.

[14] Henry Mintzberg , *The Rise and Fall of Strategic planning*, (New York:Simon and Schuster Inc., 1993), 5.

[15] Richard Whittington, *What is strategy-and does it matter?* (London: Routledge,1993), 15

[16] Paul Fifield, *Marketing Strategy*, (London: Butterworth-Heinmann, 1998),9

[17] Henry Mintzberg, "The Design School: reconsidering the basic premises of strategic management", *Strategic Management Journal,* 11,1990:176-95

[18] Richard Lynch. *Corporate Strategy* (Harlow: FT Prentice Hall, 2006),16.

[19] Richard Lynch. *Corporate Strategy* (Harlow: FT Prentice Hall, 2006), 43

[20] Writing in the 1950s, Herbert Simon was amongst the first to argue the unreliability and limitations of human decision making made Adam Smith's simjple economic assumption that humans would usually take rational decisions somewhat dubious. See March, JG and Simon H, 1958. *Organisations* , Wiley, New York

[21] See Robert Lynch. Corporate Strategy, p 44

[22] Henry Mintzberg , The Fall and Rise of Strategic planning, Harvard Business Review, pp107-114.

[23] Henry Mintzberg , pp107-114.

[24] The key commentator is Igor Ansoff, Critique of Henry Mintzberg's The Design School', *Strategic Management Journal*, 12, 1991: 449-461.

[25] Colin Giligan and Richard M.S. Wilson, *Strategic Marketing Planning* (London: Butterworth Heinemann, 2003), 53

[26] John L. Thompson. *Strategy in Action.* (London: International Thompson Business Press, 1995), 7.

[27] See Sutherland and Canwell, *Key Concepts in Strategic Management*, p263

[28] Claire Capon, Understanding Organisational Context, 2000. Harlow: Pearson Education, 8

[29] James Austin, Howard Stevenson and Jane Wei-Skillern, 'Social and Commercial Entrepreneurship: Same, Different, or Both?" *Entrepreneurship Theory and Practice*, 30, 2006:2.

[30] John Kay. *Foundations of Corporate Success*, (Oxford:Oxford University Press, 1993) 4.

[31] Peter F. Drucker, *Practice of Management*, (London: Mercury, 1961), 5.

[32] Edward Skloot, "The venture planning process." In E. Skloot (ed.) *The nonprofit entrepreneur: creating ventures to earn income.* (New York: Foundation Center, 1988.), 26.

[33] Kevin P. Kearns, *Private Sector Strategies for Social Sector Success*, p XIII.

[34] See RH Roller , "Strategy Formulation in Nonprofit Social Services Organisations: A   proposed framework." *Nonprofit management and leadership*, 7, 1996:137-153.

[35] Kent D. Miller, *Competitive Strategies of Religious Organisations*,p436

[36] Michael Porter, "Toward a dynamic theory of strategy", *Strategic Management Journal*, 12:1991:95-117.

[37] ibid p39

[33] Rodney Stark and William Bainbridge, *A Theory of Religion*, (New York: Peter Lang, 1987),42.

[39] Michael Porter, *Competitive Advantage: Creating and Sustaining Superior Performance.* (New York:Free Press, 1985), 10.

[40] See P. Zaleski and C. Zech. "The optimal size of a religious congregation: and economic theory of clubs analysis. *American Journal of Economics and Sociology*,54:1995:439-453.

[41] Kent D. Miller, referring to the works of Wuthnow, Kotter; Pfeffer and Salancik.

[42] See Roger Finke and R. Stark, *The Churching of America, 1776-1990:Winners and Losers in Our Religious Economy* (New Brunswick: Rutgers University Press, 1992),21.

[43] Although Peter Berger is often credited with bringing the market analogy

to the analysis of religion, it was Adam Smith (1759,1776) who provided insightful economic analysis of religion in his eighteenth-century writings.

[44] Peter L. Berger, *The Sacred Canopy*, (Doubleday:New York, 1967), 138.

[45] Kent D. Miller, *Competitive Strategies of Religious Organisations*, p440

[46] Lawrence R. Iannaccone 1995. Risk, rationality and religious portfolios. *Economic Inquiry*, 33: 285-289

[47] Kent D. Miller *Competitive Strategies of Religious Organisations*, p440

[48] Kent D. Miller, *Competitive Strategies of religious organisations*, 442

[49] See for example, Chavez M. Denominations as dual structures: an organisational analysis. *Sociology of religion*, 54,1993:147-169.

[50] Roger Finke, "The consequences of competition: supply-side explanations for religious change." In *Rational Choice Theory and Religion: Summary and Assessment*, Young LA ed. (New York:Routledge Presss, 1997), 45-64.

[51] Peter Brierley. *The tide is running out*, (London :Christian Research, 2000), 236

[52] Peter Brierley, *Leadership, Vision and Growing Churches*. (London :Christian Research, 2003),3

[53] Andrew Sentence, Successful leadership in a Competitive Environment, (London :Christian Research, 2003), 13.

[54] David J. Bosch, , *Transforming Mission: Paradigm Shifts in Theology of Mission*, (Maryknoll, NY:Orbis Books, 1991), 420-432.

[55] Historical account is culled from www. valuebasedmanagement.net/faq_history_value_based_management.html

[56] Robert S. Kaplan and David P. Norton, "The Balanced Scorecard: Measures that drive performance." *Harvard Business Review*, January-February 1992, 71-79.

[57] http://www.valuebasedmanagement.net/faq_shareholder_stakeholder_perspective.htm.

[58] http://www.valuebasedmanagement.net.

[59] Tom Copeland, Tim Koller and Jack Murrin (McKinsey and Company , Inc.) *Valuation: Measuring the Value of Companies* (New York:John Wiley, 2000), 3.

[60] Tom Copeland, Tim Koller and Jack Murrin (McKinsey and Company , Inc.) *Valuation: Measuring the Value of Companies* (New York:John Wiley, 2000), 54

[61] Paul R. Nevin. *Balanced Scorecard Step by Step* (New York:John Wiley & Sons, Inc., 2002), 22.

4

Christian Managerial Perspectives

The various perspectives in the field of strategic management show the variety of pluralism. The point is well made that much rational analysis of strategy is governed by a normative compulsion to prescribe but students of process and practice share an interest in a close-up examination of how strategy is accomplished, as contrasted with the arm's-length specification of the forces that are conceived in rational analysis.[1] For example, to understand the value managers place on strategic thinking, it is needful to isolate key value-creating activities and then find the perceptions of specific group of informants.[2] Such qualitative and phenomenological approach provides insights and an understanding of people's perspectives.[3]

Good science is good conversation

The various perspectives in the strategy field are all based on different theories and base disciplines and the lack of disciplined methodology has caused fragmentation in strategic management.[4] Many concepts tend to be ambiguous, there is no clarity on definitions and theories and checklists are seldom tested or compared with competing theories. While the field has benefited from inductive research, the strictly hypothetical-deductive approach flourishes best in 'harder' theories like 'agency theory', 'game theory', 'industrial organisation' and 'decision theory'.

It is also argued that within strategic management, it is by developing dominant research programmes like the traditional 'competitive forces' perspective or the 'resource-based' perspectives that progress could be made.[5] In addition to the disciplined methodological and dominant research programme approaches is the more pragmatic but opposing approach of methodological pluralism which is based on the notion that 'good science is good conversation'.[6] This position is premised on the view that the use of the disciplined methodological and dominant research programme approaches employ a strongly instrumental approach which excludes new insights that do not fit within a hard theory or dominant research programme.

Furthermore, these so-called harder sciences face the same problems in the sense that the concepts are often ambiguous and not clearly defined too. Instead of looking for universal methodological criteria the continual attunement of rivalling perspectives in strategic management should be promoted. [7]

Managerial perspectives

Many more theoretical (and even practical) lenses are needed to explore the range of issues that the strategy field offers[8]. This section highlights some of the perspectives of UK Christian strategic managers.[9, 10]

Meaning of strategic thinking

Christian strategic managers define strategic thinking both in terms of thinking, planning and acting with long term insight in the light of current development and as ideas and reflections to get to grips with issues to generate breakthroughs.

> *Many more theoretical and practical lenses are needed to explore the range of issues that the strategy field offers.*

Reasons for Applying Strategic thinking

Christian strategic managers apply strategic thinking for a variety of reasons which include grasping the bigger picture, having a long-term view, generating insight to move their organisations forward during change and scanning the environment to identify opportunities or disruptive change.

Ways of applying strategic thinking

Managers apply strategic thinking both within formal and informal planning processes.

The value of strategic thinking

There are three key areas where managers perceive value is generated when strategic thinking is applied. These are thought value, organisational value and economic value.

Thought value. The application of strategic thinking encourages managers to think when they otherwise would not. Most importantly, it helps them to think creatively, thinking about the possible and imagining the future.

Organisational value. Strategic managers add value to their organisations when they apply strategic thinking as it helps them to clarify their options and priorities. The application of strategic thinking leads to the effective implementation and allocation of resources and is a primer for envisioning and action, that is, converting mission statements into reality.

Economic value of strategic thinking. Strategic thinking potentially adds economic value either through indirectly making managers and the organisation more effective or directly challenging managers to take a hard look at their organisations' finances. The importance of strategic thinking lies in the fact that it helps managers make effective use of gifts, resources and stakeholder support.

Applying strategic thinking

Enabling factors. Strategic thinking is facilitated when it is integrated into implementation rather being seen as 'blue-sky and when it is part of the organisation's mindset.

Constraining factors. Factors constraining the way strategic managers apply strategic thinking show that lack of time to engage in strategic thinking is the major challenge. Also, the application of strategic thinking is constrained when it is not embedded in the culture of the organisation.

Getting more value from strategic thinking. Managerial views on what could be done to get more value from strategic thinking include: communicating the specific value of strategic thinking to managers and the organisation, crafting strategic thoughts into an economically valuable form, tailoring key concepts of strategic thinking and practicing what is preached about strategic thinking.

Strategic thinking and strategic planning
While strategic thinking is defined in terms of thinking and planning with long term insight in the light of current development, there are perceptions of potential differences on the elements of strategic thinking and strategic planning.

Delivering value
Perspectives on the values that Christian organisations seek to deliver, in order of importance are spiritual value, social value and financial value.

The purpose of strategy
The purpose for using strategy includes, in order of importance, spiritual value, organisational value, social value, thought value and financial value.

Stakeholder analysis
The stakeholders of the Christian organisation, in order of importance are God, staff and members, clients and donors.

Strategic thinking is used to address strategic issues posed by the distinct organisational context and it adds value a huge diversity of ways. In some ways, this is similar to business organisations, where in addition to economic value, the value added by strategic thinking can also come from business value (for example as deliberate strategy, emergent strategy, or through change), thought value (through creating alignment within managers' thoughts), soft value (through building confidence, reducing anxiety, and through building appropriately focused excitement) and prioritisation (through a very clear strategic thinking process).[11]

Christian organisations seek to deliver, in order of importance, spiritual value, social value and financial value

Strategic thinking is used to address strategic issues posed by the distinct organisational context and it adds value in a huge diversity of ways.

NOTES

[1] Mahmoud Ezzamel and Hugh Willmott. Rethinking strategy: contemporary perspectives and debates. *European Management Review*, 1, 2004:44

[2] Tony Grundy and Laura Brown, *Be Your Own Strategy Consultant: Demystifying Strategic Thinking* (London: Thomson Learning,2002), 228.

[3] Paul D. Leedy and Jeanne Ellis Omrod, *Practical Research Planning and Design* (2001), 153.

[4] C. Camera. Redirecting research in business policy and strategy. *Strategic Management Journal*, 6, 1985:1-15.

[5] See D.C. Teece. Contributions and impediments of economic analysis to the study of strategic management. In J.W. Fredrickson (ed). *Perspectives on strategic management.* (New York: Harper and Row, 1990), 39-80.

[6] See T.J. Mahoney. Strategic management and determinism: sustaining the conversation. *Journal of Management Studies*, 30, 1993:173-191.

[7] See T.J. Mahoney. Strategic management and determinism: sustaining the conversation. *Journal of Management Studies*, 30, 1993:173-191.

[8] See for example, Combatoir K. Prahalad and Gary Hamel. Strategy as a field of study: why search for a new paradigm? *Strategic Management Journal*, 15, 1994:5-16

[9] See Kwaku Ahenkora. Strategy, context and value creation: Perspectives of UK strategic managers on strategy, the organisational purpose and contextual value added. Unpublished PhD dissertation. Trinity College, Newburgh.2007.

[10] Peter Brierley. *Coming up Trumps. Four Ways into the Future* (Milton Keynes : Authentic Media, 2004).

[11] Tony Grundy and Laura Brown, *Be Your Own Strategy Consultant: Demystifying Strategic Thinking* (London: Thomson Learning,2002),158.

5

Christian Concepts

Christian managerial perspectives provide opportunity to understand the role of the organisation's distinctive purpose in shaping strategic management concepts such as 'strategic intent', 'value creation', 'strategic thinking', the 'ideology of strategy' and 'strategizing'; .

Strategic intent

An effective strategic management starts from a deep understanding of the context, both of the enterprise itself and the external environment of the organisation. The organisational context is usually associated with the external environment, but the precise role and purpose of nonprofit organisations actually define the environment in which they exist and with whom it is engaged.[1]

The Purpose of the organisation

Strategic intent is the highest-level purpose of the organisation. What is the purpose of the organisation and what is the purpose for strategy? Christian organisations exist to deliver spiritual value, organisational value and social value. The term 'spiritual value' sums up the view that the Christian organisations exist primarily to serve individuals seeking Christian spirituality.

Social perspective to strategic intent

The overriding mission of the Christian organisation is the guiding principle for strategic intent, providing the psychological contract, the sense of direction and destiny for all the stakeholders. One of the key issues for strategic management is the confusion over the subjectivity and coherence of strategic intent, that is, who has strategic intent in an organisation and how is coherence of strategic intent maintained within the organisation or institution.[2] Strategic intent was originally created as a concept for a business managerial audience but the concept has been taken up in academic discourse other than business strategy.[3] There are three key aspects of an effective strategic intent:

1. **Sense of Direction**. Strategic intent implies a particular point of view about the long-term market or competitive position that a firm hopes to build over the coming decade or so. It should be a view of the future – conveying a unifying and personalising sense of direction.

2. **Sense of Discovery**. A strategic intent is differentiated; it implies a competitively unique point of view about the future. It holds out to employees the promise of exploring new competitive territory.

3. **Sense of Destiny**. Strategic intent has an emotional edge to it; it is a goal that employees perceive as inherently worthwhile.

The managerial role of strategic intent is to go beyond environment-sensitive strategic planning to represent objectives "for which one cannot plan". As such, strategic intent represents a proactive mode in strategizing, a symbol of the organisation's will about the future, which energizes all organisational levels for a collective purpose. Strategic intent also reflects the 'corporate context' in which bottom-up business ideas are weighed, directs the accumulation of necessary competencies and gives the intra-organisational change processes a common target, "something to 'aim' for".[4,5]

Strategic intent is therefore a useful concept in accounting for purpose and continuity of goals in an organisation adapting to internal and external evolutionary pressures; not just for large multinational corporations, in which context it was originally presented but also for smaller organisations. However, 'intent' is a psychological concept which is possessed by a conscious actor.[6] Organisations are not conscious and cannot possess intent in a strict sense, i.e., organisational intent needs to be possessed by some or all of its members. The use of the term 'organisational intent' runs the risk of obscuring who the actor possessing strategic intent is. Organisations are often pluralistic and fragmented, which underlines the necessity to be explicit regarding subjectivity when addressing mental phenomena on the organisational level of analysis.

The sense of submission to super-ordinate mission and higher purpose, evident in the delivery of spiritual value, creates the superarching mindset of the Christian enterprise. The organisation's dedication to a compelling long-range shared vision (intent) is a critical success factor in generating the internal consensus and fervour needed for innovation and change.[7] Creating such organisational intent to achieve the future requires strong moral leadership and an empowering cultural process that reaches deep into management ranks.[8] The inherent challenges of generating such a consensus of purpose makes the shared organisational vision a rare (firm-specific) resource, and few organisations have been able to establish or maintain a widely or enduring sense of mission to achieve that vision.[9]

Institutional theorists argue that organisations exist in relation to other similar organisations: accountancy firms are similar, universities are similar, publishing firms are similar and so on.[10] Over time similarities develop in terms of the way people in those organisations see their organisations and the environment in which the organisation operates, including the nature of customers, suppliers, competitors and so on. They also have ways of doing things that tend to be similar. These ways of seeing the world and ways of doing things can be so taken for granted, so institutionalised, it is difficult for people to question or change them; they can come to be seen as the legitimate way to behave within an industry, so organisational strategies tend to develop within institutionally similar cultural parameters.[11]

The higher purpose of the Christian organisation- strategic intent, is prescriptive and gives direction and a sense of destiny to the organisation- an enterprise whose distinctive purpose is to create, maintain, and exchange supernatural compensators and rewards.[12]

Contextual Value Added

Strategic thinking is used to deliver spiritual value, followed by organisational value, social value, thought value and then financial value. This emanates from the organisational purpose to deliver primarily spiritual and social values. Strategy is a means to an end; the purpose for strategy follows the intended organisational purpose. Clearly,

Christian social enterprise organisations generate value-adding activities that have a clear purpose and need strategies to attain that purpose. Managers think strategically and make strategic choices that involve deciding what action to take and how to take it for the future of their organisations.

Strategic thinking is used to address strategic issues posed by the distinct organisational context in a way that fits with the strategic intent and that also adds value to the organisation in a huge diversity of ways. The core business of religious organisations is the provision of supernatural compensators that is generally bundled with temporal rewards. While the strategic purpose of the business organisation is usually simplified to profit maximisation and survival, the purpose of the Christian social enterprise organisation is multifaceted; purpose is complex, involving not only profit and survival but also the motivations of the people involved and the relationship of the organisation with society and the community.[13] The distinction between social and commercial enterprise is not dichotomous, but rather more accurately conceptualized as a continuum ranging from purely social to purely economic.[14] Even at the extremes, however, there are still elements of both. That is, charitable activity must still reflect economic realities, while economic activity must still generate social value.

Every organisation, whether private company, public body or charity, needs to develop its purpose and develop a common understanding of the main elements. Key elements integral to the purpose of the Christian social enterprise organisation are spiritual value, social value, financial value, and organisational value. That is, in addition to broad purpose, generating value-added spiritual service is of prime importance.

The use of strategy to ensure survival is not limited to commercial enterprises. What do we have to do to stay in business? This question, in the Christian context, has nothing whatsoever to do with commercial business, but rather thinking of 'business' as 'retaining a sense of identity and purpose for the institution. [15] Part of the answer is to have a vision and a strategy for fulfilling it and the other part lies in identifying the invisible component that successfully creates the conditions for the strategy to be fulfilled: it is to the invisible to which strategic thinking in Christian organizations must rise and define. The Will, Word and Work of the invisible God, whose key purpose is to further the Kingdom of

God, is the guiding purpose for the Christian organisation. [16]

> *The Will, Word and Work of the invisible God, whose key purpose is to further the Kingdom of God, is the guiding purpose for the Christian organisation*

Strategic thinking or strategy delivers value in context for strategic purpose must align with organisational purpose. A different view on managing for value creation in business requires a focus on long-run cash flow returns and the willingness to adopt a dispassionate, value-oriented view of corporate activities that recognises businesses for what they are- investments in new productive capacity that either earn a return above their opportunity cost of capital or do not.[17] Ability to manage value is an essential part of developing sound corporate and business strategies- strategies that create value for shareholders and maintain an advantage in the market for corporate control. A focus on managing value does not mean creating value through financial manipulation; rather it means creating value through developing sound strategic and operational plans for a company's businesses. The link between sound strategy and value creation is a tight one.

However, from the systemic perspective of strategy, economic activity cannot be placed in a separate sphere of impersonal financial calculation because of our social embeddedness.[18] What this means is that economic behaviour is embedded in a network of social relations; families, the state, professions. These networks influence both the means and the ends of action, defining what is appropriate and reasonable behaviour for their members. Thus, personal histories which include educational background, religion, gender, family position, and ethnicity all shape economic activity. This social constructivist view suggests that the norms which guide strategy are not cognitive but cultural.[19] Culture, defined as a series of social systems, effects and is affected by firms, industries and economies.

> *Strategic thinking or strategy delivers value in context, for strategic purpose must align with organisational purpose.*

Strategic management can exist in a particular context that is unique for the enterprise. The context, as previously noted, consists of different features- both of the enterprise itself (internal environment) and the external environment. The distinctive purpose of the Christian social enterprise plays a part in determining the issues which strategic management must address and hence the agenda and scope of strategic management for the organisation. The context dependency of value creation warrants the use of the term 'contextual value added' for social enterprise organisations whose ultimate purpose for creating value is not purely economic value. Thus, the high-level purpose of the organisation provides the incentives for perceived value added.

Traditionally, the measurement of business value has been financial. However, the reliance on financial measures of performance has come under criticism in recent years with critics suggesting that financial measures are not consistent with today's business environment, lack predictive power, reinforce functional silos, may sacrifice long-term thinking, and are not relevant to many levels of organisation.[20] Financial metrics better serve as a means of reporting on the stewardship of funds entrusted to management's care rather than charting the future direction of the organisation. Financial measures tend to focus on short-term results, often at the expense of long-term value-creating activities. It has been suggested that approximately 75 percent of an organisation's value is derived from intangible assets.[21] These assets are different from the traditional view in that they may not have a direct impact on financial results, they represent largely potential value, and they require interdependence. Managers of Christian social enterprises, therefore, are stewards of financial resources and that strategy adds value beyond the financial metrics.

> *The term 'contextual value added' is useful for social enterprise organisations whose ultimate purpose for creating value is not purely economic value but multifaceted.*

The Balanced Scorecard aptly balances the historical accuracy and integrity of financial numbers with the drivers of future success.[22] It was originally conceived with for-profit organisations in mind but has been adopted by many public and nonprofit sector institutions. Observations on results of ten years of learning and research into a large number of companies that implemented the Scorecard showed that most nonprofits and government organisations had difficulty with the original architecture, where the financial perspective was placed at the top of the hierarchy.[23] Given that achieving financial success is not the primary objective for most of these organisations, the architecture had to be rearranged to place customers or constituents at the top of the hierarchy (the four quadrants of the balanced scorecard are financial, customer, internal processes and employee learning and growth).

In this context, the measures on the scorecard should link together to drive the organisation's mission; this differs from the for-profit model in which all measures ultimately lead to improved financial performance.[24] In fact, nonprofit agencies place an overarching objective at the top of their scorecard that represents their long-term objective. Other objectives within the scorecard are oriented toward improving such a high-level objective.

For a private sector company, financial measures provide accountability to the owners, the shareholders but for a nonprofit organisation, the financial measures are not the relevant indicators of whether the organisation is delivering on its mission. The organisation's mission should be featured and measured at the highest level of its scorecard. Placing an overarching objective on the scorecard for a nonprofit organisation clearly communicates the organisation's long-term mission. The reconfiguring of the balanced scorecard to incorporate the unique context of nonprofit organisations shows the importance of re-tooling strategy for different contexts.

It is in keeping with this that the concept of 'contextual value added' in the strategic management lexicon becomes meaningful as a measure of value that captures the perceived value of strategy in the nonprofit organisational or social enterprise context. The concept acknowledges that focus on value creation is a necessity for nonprofit organisations, but also recognises that value and its measure must be contextualised for the nonprofit strategic manager.

Stakeholders and strategic purpose

With regards to the purpose of the Christian social enterprise organisation, the stakeholder value perspective is the framework for strategic managing. The shareholder perspective is the prevalent thinking of commercial enterprises. With this perspective the purpose of the organisation is to advance the interests of its shareholders, the owners. Typically, this means that organisational purpose is defined in terms of increasing the wealth of the shareholders. With such an approach to purpose, the problem is often the separation between ownership by the shareholders and control of the enterprise by its senior managers. [25] As companies grow larger, two trends emerge; shareholdings become more widespread and diffuse, so giving individual shareholders less power; managers, however, gain control over large range of assets and acquire increasingly greater remuneration and power-purpose shifts.[26]

The non-distributive restriction on surpluses generated by nonprofit organisations and the embedded social purpose limits their use of capital markets. Additionally, the economics of a social entrepreneurial venture often makes it difficult to compensate staff as competitively as in commercial markets.[27] Some employees in social entrepreneurial organisations place considerable value on non-pecuniary compensation from their work.

The social purpose of the social sector manager creates greater challenges for measuring performance than the commercial business manager who can rely on relatively tangible and quantifiable measures of performance such as financial indicators, market share, customer satisfaction, and quality. Additionally, the various financial and non-financial stakeholders to which the social enterprise is readily accountable to are greater in number and more varied, resulting in greater complexity in managing these relationships. [28] The challenge of measuring social change is great due to non-quantifiability, multi-causality, temporal dimensions, and perceptive differences of the social impact created.

It must be recognised that in the early days of framing the subject matter of the academic discipline of strategic management, strategy was defined as a pattern of purposes and policies. One of the major shifts in thinking about the purpose of strategy in recent years has been the increasing emphasis placed upon shareholder value. The shareholder-agency model of the organisation influences the trends of business practice, but there are suggestions that commercial enterprises should take a look at the alternative view of the firm as a social institution, and the manager's role as trustee not agent. .[29]

The duty of the trustee is to preserve and enhance, to balance the expectations of a range of stakeholders, employees, customers and suppliers, the company's reputation in the community, and not just the interests of the shareholder. The agency model expects the manager to attach priority to the current shareholder interests, the trustee has to balance the conflicting interests of current stakeholders and additionally to weigh the interests of present and future stakeholders.[30] The proper responsibility of the strategic manager is to build a good and successful business, one that earns good returns to its investors, has a capable and motivated workforce, enjoys a fine reputation with its customers and the community, and is regarded by its suppliers as a good, if tough, firm to do business with. What prevails in practice, however, is the inexorable move towards the agency model that is at odds, at least in its espoused rhetoric of shareholder value as the major managerial concern, with the sense of responsibility. In this context, management faces growing pressure to improve corporate earnings via restructuring, cost-cutting, divestments, to enhance their investment status and the salaries of top management. The pressure to perform according to this model is global.

However, in the business context, the devastating effect- unrestrained pursuit of self-interest, market fundamentalism, minimal state interference in business- is directly at odds with the relationships that allow markets to function effectively. The shareholder-agency model does not necessarily take into account social value and this decline of the social capital has been accompanied by a spate of corporate scandals and by widely perceived abuse of management knowledge and power.[31] There is urgent need, therefore, to be far clearer on the purposes we espouse and the values that support them.

In today's world, for nonprofits to transform lofty aspirations into quantifiable impact, they need to become more familiar with traditional business tools. However, such tools must be adapted to the espoused purposes of social enterprises who uphold the stakeholder perspective. With social enterprises' espoused purpose of delivering social value, business organisations may learn from nonprofits. The challenge still remains; to build economic institutions that are based on a mutuality of obligation within civil society, to link our personal and work lives to questions of the good of society, because the country is becoming less of a good place to live, the social capital which all rely on to build wellbeing and the good life is diminishing.[32]

It is helpful to analyse, and understand the expectations of different stakeholders and the extent to which they are likely to show an active interest in the strategic development of the organisation or seek to exercise an influence over its purpose and strategies.[33] In the Christian context, God is the stakeholder with controlling interest whose perspectives shape the ultimate purpose of the organisation. The perceived highest-level purpose of the Christian organisation, the delivery of spiritual and social values, is a unifying umbrella that shapes the broad ends that the Christian institution seeks. Different stakeholders will affect or be affected by the organisation in diverse ways, hence stakeholders would have different interests or stakes in the organisation. Stakeholders with high power and high interest are key players in the organisation and are often involved in managing the organisation and its future.[34]   Even if key players are not directly involved in managing the organisation, then it is vital that they are given serious consideration in the development of long-term plans and the future direction of the organisation, as they have the power to block proposed plans.

Nurturing strategic thinking

This section clarifies some of the salient issues surrounding the concept of strategic thinking. For example, how do strategic thinking and strategic planning fit within the same strategic management regime and what are the key elements based on the Christian managerial perspective?

Strategic thinking or strategic planning

Strategic thinking is perceived in terms of thinking, planning and acting with long term insight in the light of current development and also as ideas and reflections to get to grips with issues to generate breakthroughs. Strategic thinking is, therefore, used foremost to generate insight to move organisations forward. While the application of the concept may sound confusing, in terms of blurring distinctions between strategic thinking and planning, there are potential differences. The lack of clear understanding about what is meant by the term strategic thinking has led to considerable confusion in the strategic management field.[35] The differences between strategic thinking and planning emerge from the key words used to describe strategic thinking- 'futuristic thinking', 'thinking about ends', 'wide ranging', 'creative thinking' and strategic planning- 'crystallising ideas', 'practical steps'.

Strategic planning and strategic thinking may well be described as different sides of the same coin and each on its own is necessary, but not sufficient for an effective strategic management framework for it is daft to engage in strategic planning before undertaking strategic thinking.[36] Strategic thinking has to be wide ranging; outside the box; spanning past and present; lateral thinking; moving into the future.[37] In earlier attempts to differentiate between the two, traditional approaches to planning was described as 'form filling' while strategic thinking was referred to as 'crafting strategic architecture'.[38] Strategic thinking is merely thinking about strategy but improvement in strategic planning has profoundly changed the character of strategic planning so it is more appropriate to refer to it as strategic management or strategic thinking. [39]

In sharp contrast to this view, strategic thinking is not merely 'alternative nomenclature for everything falling under the umbrella of strategic management, but rather it is a particular way of thinking with specific and clearly discernible characteristics.[40] The differences are that strategic planning is the systematic programming of pre-identified strategies from which an action plan is developed while strategic thinking is a synthesising process utilising intuition and creativity whose outcome is an integrated perspective of the enterprise. The dichotomy between the creative versus the analytic is pervasive in the discussions on the subject of strategic thinking and strategic planning.[41]

The Christian managerial viewpoint that strategic thinking is wide ranging could be likened to that of the systems' perspective where the strategic thinker has a mental model of the complete system of value creation from beginning to end, and understands the interdependencies within the chain. [42] Mental models influence behaviour and new insights fail to get put into practice because they conflict with deeply held internal images of how the world works, images that limit us to familiar ways of thinking and acting.[43] Furthermore, the mental model of how the world works must incorporate an understanding of both the external and internal context of the organisation and must lead to the perception of an organisation in a context larger than that of the industry. Thus, in addition to understanding the external business ecosystem in which the organisation operates, strategic thinkers must also appreciate the organisational purpose and the inter-relationships among various stakeholders and other individual internal parts that, together, constitute the whole, because the whole is greater than the sum of its parts.

Other descriptive terms are 'futuristic thinking' and 'thinking about ends'. Strategic thinking is therefore 'purpose-driven' or 'intent-focused'. As previously pointed out strategic intent implies a particular point of view about the long-term market or competitive position that a firm hopes to build over the coming decade or so and it conveys a sense of direction, discovery, and destiny. Strategic intent also provides the focus that allows individuals within an organisation to marshal and leverage their energy, to focus attention, to resist distraction, and to concentrate for as long as it takes to achieve a goal. [44] From this perspective, the real question is not what does the future the organisation is trying to create look like, rather it is having seen the future that is to be created, what must be kept from that past, lose from that past, and create in the present, to get there. This can be referred to as 'thinking in time'- thinking that spans the past, present and future.

Strategic thinkers in Christian organisations in the United Kingdom are known to have the ability to think widely, spanning past, present and future and have the capacity to think laterally and often outside the box.[45] In this regard, strategic thinking connects the past, present, and future and uses the organisation's purpose and historical context as critical inputs into the creation of its future. The elements of strategic thinking describe a strategic thinker with a broad field view that sees the whole and the connections between its pieces, both across the vertical levels of strategy and the horizontal elements of the end-to-end value system.

Questions have been raised in the strategic management literature about the compatibility of strategic thinking with strategic planning. A useful suggestion is that strategic thinking is thinking about the longer term and the more important ends in any situation; if and when one identifies such an end or set of ends, and choose among the possible pathways the ones that make most sense, the process of corporate planning can get under way.[46] A similar perspective explains that the purpose of strategic thinking is to discover novel, imaginative strategies which can re-write the rules of the competitive game and to envision potential futures, significantly different from the present.[47] The purpose of strategic planning is to operationalise the strategies developed through strategic thinking and to support the strategic thinking process. Strategic thinking and strategic planning are therefore interrelated in a dialectical process, where both are necessary for effective strategic management, and each on its own is necessary but not sufficient. The tools that one uses at each stage of the strategic management process are not important in themselves but as the means of encouraging the creative and analytical mindset. There ideally needs to be a dialectical thought process of being able to diverge and then converge, being creative and then seeing the real-world implications, and being synthetic but also analytical.

A broadened view of the strategy-making process incorporates both strategic thinking and strategic planning as related activities, each valuable in its own right in an ongoing process of creating and disrupting the alignment between an organisation's present and its future. For example, both academics and practitioners have embraced the McKinsey "7S Model" that aligns strategy, structure, systems, super-ordinate goals, staff, skills, and shared values, because it is recognised that purposeful, efficient organisational action cannot be taken if these factors work at cross-purposes with each other. The dilemma is that unaligned, these factors work at cross-purposes; aligned they drive out potentially needed change. An appropriately reconstituted strategy making framework would build in the possibility of institutionalising a process that continually examines the tension between the creation of the alignment necessary to support efficiency and effectiveness and the disruption of alignment necessary to foster change and adaptability.

Strategic thinking disrupts alignment by creating a gap in the minds of managers of today's reality and a more desirable future. This, in turn, opens the gap that is the driving force behind strategy-making aimed at change. Translating the strategic intent into new institutional behaviours, however, necessitates strategic planning, that is, the realignment of structures, systems, processes, and skills around the new intent in a way that begins to close the gap that strategic thinking opens. Thus, strategic thinking and strategic planning may work in tandem within the same strategic management framework. [48]

Enabling factors

Strategic thinking is perceived to be highly facilitated when it is part of the organisations mindset and also when it is linked to implementation. Based on the potential of strategic thinking to add value, organisations need to explicitly communicate that strategic thinking is something which can and should be done at all levels and where boundaries are erected, they must be justified.[49] The potential value of strategic thinking is dissipated by softer constraints such as organisational thinking style, mindset and lack of direct personal pay-offs of doing it. Strategy is frequently not implemented as it is often perceived as relatively intangible and qualitative. To create organisational capacity for strategic thinking that meets the fundamental tests for strategically valuable positive outcomes, there must be the accompanying supporting strategic planning context to encourage and enable the implementation of the fruits of this type of thinking. [50]

Constraining factors

The lack of time to engage in strategic thinking, as well as the need to embed strategic thinking into the culture of the organisation, is a major challenge. Also in crisis, the organisation feels under pressure from present challenges and turns in on itself, and cannot look too far into the future. Nonetheless, firms who succeed at embedding a capability for strategic thinking throughout their organisations create a new source of competitive advantage. [51] Their whole (holistic) system perspective should allow them to redesign their processes for greater efficiency and effectiveness. Their intent-focus will make them more determined and less distracted than their rivals. Their ability to think in time will improve the quality of their decision-making and speed of implementation.

Getting more value from strategic thinking

Getting more value from strategic thinking requires communicating the specific value to managers and tailoring the key concepts of strategic thinking to the needs of the organisation; most importantly establishing the 'theological' basis of strategic management. Researchers and leaders continue to find answers to the question why few Church leaders think and plan in a long-term visionary and strategic way. The answer is attributed in part to the allergy that many of the leaders have towards insights from leadership and management practice [52], and partly to the absence of the Christian managerial and theological perspectives on strategic management. The development of contextual insights into strategic management minimises the allergy that Christian strategic managers have from 'secular' strategic management concepts.

The management of strategy

Christian strategic managers develop and apply strategic thinking both through formal and informal planning processes. Some of the informal ways of applying strategic thinking include 'flashes of insights', 'intuitive knowledge and foresight, prayer and spiritual insight'. One view of strategic management is, indeed, that strategy should be managed through rational planning processes in the form of sequence of steps involving setting objectives, the analysis of environmental trends and resource capabilities, continuing through the evaluation of different options, and ending with the careful planning of the strategy implementation.[53] The underlying principle is that strategies are the outcome of careful objective analyses and planning, and in this way managers are able to establish the future directions of their organisations. However, not all organisations have them, and even when they do, it would be a mistake to assume that strategies of organisations necessarily come about through them.

The management of strategy is also thought of as a process of 'crafting'.[54] Here strategic management is seen not as a formal planning process, but rather in terms of processes by which strategies develop in organisations on the basis of managers' experiences, their sensitivity to changes in their environment and what they learn from operating in their markets. This does not mean that managers are not thinking about the strategic position of their organisation, or the choices it faces, but that it may not be taking place in a highly formalised way such as through planning systems.[55]

That intuition and 'spiritual' sensitivity are potential drivers of strategy in the Christian organisational context is worth considering. Complexity and chaos theory argue that the world in which organisations exist is highly complex and unpredictable and it is inconceivable that managers can know all there is to know about this complexity, let alone predict its effects specifically.[56] However, people's experience within a particular context can help them become sensitive to the complexity and uncertainty around them. They do this by becoming familiar with patterns in the complexity and uncertainty. When there are deviations from these patterns they are able to sense them intuitively. Strategic managers should develop their capacity to be intuitive and take action based on that.[57] Christian strategic managers do not only exercise intuition but also spiritual sensitivity and take actions based on such insights.

The ideology of strategy

Clarifying the theological basis of strategic thinking and applying the relevant concepts in the field are means of making strategy more useful to Christian social enterprise strategic managers. The strategic intent and stakeholder perspectives show the strategic importance of the underlying values and ideology. Values, expectations and ideologies of different stakeholder groups play an important part in the development of strategy. [58] This is particularly the case where the purpose of the organisation is rooted in such values. The fundamental purpose of the Christian organisation is rooted in its spiritual foundation. While the purpose and mission are heavily theological the vision is mixed: some characteristics of vision are theological and some engage practical needs and problems.[59] Theology or Christian ideology plays a role in the development of strategy in the Christian organisational context.

Naturally, this opens up the stalled debate in strategic management on the question, 'Is strategic management ideological? A critique of the academic strategic management field addressed the need to examine unstated managerial values and assumptions and to generate less ideologically value-laden and more universal knowledge about strategic management of organisations.[60] The five operational criteria used to assess the ideological nature of strategic management research were: the factual under-determination of action norms; the universalisation of sectional interests; denial of conflict and contradiction; normative idealization of sectional goals; and the naturalization of the status quo. Against these criteria strategic management tends to be ideological. The critique implies that the 'field' supports repressive managerial practice and legitimises real inequalities in organisational life.

There are two important contributions to the critical analysis of strategic management. One view is strategy as praxis, the other is how ideology works at a conscious level through the manipulation of communication and at an institutional level through ideas which favour dominant interests. When strategic management is conceptualised as praxis, that is, practice informed by theoretical considerations, this fosters the acquisition of communicative competence by all subjects that allows them to participate in discourse aimed at liberation from constraints on interaction. The idea of praxis is important in that it recognizes that managers are not acting alone, but are supported by a range of ideas, theories, models and schemes which are generated for them by strategic 'theorists' of various types, including consultants and academics. However, academic ideas need to be scrutinized every bit as much as strategic practices because of the ideological basis of many mainstream contributions to the strategy field. [61] The analysis of ideology shows communication and ideas as the two main components of ideology. Although the inter-relationship of discourse (communication) and ideas is not fully explored, they might be closely linked.[62]

The ideological nature and the discourse of strategic management have implication for the application of traditional strategic management concepts to the Christian social enterprise organisation. In this context, purpose is theological and it influences the overarching ideology. Attempts to link the fields of organisation studies and strategy show that the very language, symbols and exchanges around the subject of strategy have important outcomes.[63] For example, Christian management writers differ on purpose and mission; they are viewed as separate or the same and thus different uses of words are used to discuss similar concepts, leading to different approaches to strategic management. [64]

The concern of discursive analysis is to better appreciate how, as forms of power-knowledge, strategy talk and texts, are actively involved in the constitution of what, for example, rational and processual models of strategy contrive to prescribe or describe.[65] Respected management writers accounts of strategy, therefore, are credible and valuable within their own terms of reference. Some writers, for example, see corporate strategy as a set of discourses and practices which transform managers and employees alike into subjects who secure their sense of purpose and reality by formulating, evaluating and conducting strategy.[66] Towards this end, managers cannot stand outside of ideology to impose their dominant ideology on unwitting workers, because they are also entangled in discursive webs. Strategy constructs a myth of commonality of organisational purpose by positing lofty and unattainable aspirations.

The application of strategic management concepts, therefore, requires a close-up examination of the organisational purpose, stakeholder expectation and idealogies. Strategy or strategic management is conventionally studied as a distinctive field of activity that exists independently of efforts to specify its features and/or prescribe for its perfection- discursive analysis. Strategy as discouse is intimately involved in constituting the intentions and actions from which it is thought to be derived. [67] Strategy, then, is an integral part, and not independent, of the actions or practices that is frequently drawn upon to explain or justify. Thus, an examination of the ideological nature of strategic management requires an analysis of, not only structures of organisational domination, but also practices and events, which are largely discursive. Discourse is not inherently ideological, but becomes ideologically invested within different social and institutional settings.[68]

The implication of this for strategic management is that we must examine: how ideas and discourses are produced, by whom and in what context; how the resulting texts are distributed and consumed; how they are interpreted and then drawn into discursive practices within organisations; and in turn how those practices are interpreted. The discourse approach systematises the notion that organisations are dominated by words, written texts, conversations and stories, even to the point at which 'strategy must rank as one of the most prominent, influential, and costly stories told in organisations.'[69] Both talk and text are a condition and consequence of a particular context and it is this relevance to their context that renders any talk and text plausible.[70]

The ideological basis of strategic management is always in a flux, likely to change, so we are therefore faced with analysing a moving target and building strategies on shifting concepts.[71] In an attempt to 'make sense' of the strategic management literature, and specifically the place of Porter and his ideologies within it, an interpretative research was undertaken on the search for a strategic management narrative.[72] The question, what is strategic management? often leads to the work of Porter. This is because strategic management texts inevitably contain his models, theories and frameworks which imply that they are 'fundamental' to the field. However, an historical journey through six prominent management journals shows that he was not a constant contributor; in fact he is almost absent from the journals, but his work is often the study of empirical testing or theoretical debate. Although his prescriptions for generic strategies are difficult to implement, generic strategies remain the enacted discourse of choice by senior managers. [73] To attempt implementation managers require a sense of 'reality' which is based on the effects of 'forgetting, neglecting or denying the subjectivity' which is the condition necessary to render the generic strategies possible.

The problem with Porter's framework is that if every business adopted the strategies advocated, none would be able to secure a competitive advantage. However, the promise of 'unequal power' which is derived from 'specialist knowledge' located in the promises which cannot be fulfilled continues to be supported by senior management the world over. It is argued that Porter's work is attractive to management precisely because this expert knowledge provides 'some illusion of control, legitimacy and security in the face of uncertainty; thus reinforcing the view that strategic management could be considered an ideological myth. [74]

There are indications that some of the noblest of human achievements are myths created to give a sense of permanence and that each generation creates or assumes its own 'unattainable but approachable goals' in the form of a myth. The function of the myth is to 'provide a criterion' against which all purposes can be judged' even though the multiplicity of purposes cannot be expressed in the myth. However, to be 'acceptable and effective' a myth must meet the Beeby criteria.[75]:

- There must be a 'general accord' with some strong if not clearly defined, aspiration
- The myth must be expressed in language sufficiently flexible to permit a reasonably wide range of interpretations
- The language of the myth must allow the possibility of providing practical guidance
- And most importantly, the myth must be 'unattainable in the near future' so that it may be sustainable through 'consistent change'
- The final paradox is that the people working under the myth must believe in it so completely that they will fight for it in its youth, must hold to it in its middle age, but be prepared to see another myth set up in its place when it has served its purpose.

'Strategic management ' and 'strategy', even 'competitive strategy' all seem to meet the criteria of a myth. 'Strategy' is the word of choice even though it has a range of interpretations. Practical guidance abounds in the literature, but somehow 'new and improved' models exist to keep the field in constant motion. The classical conception of strategy as espoused by Porter may not always fit comfortably in other cultures.[76] However, a discourse based on an American business culture which respects profit, values technical procedures and regards the free market as an article of faith has to be taken seriously. It does not matter whether formal planning as prescribed by the Classical school is economically efficient. If that is how the institutional players expect business to be done, then it is sociologically efficient to play the game. It may be that the rationality of the Classical approach to strategy is only a social construction, but as it is presently the dominant construction, it is difficult to ignore.

As noted, in the Christian organisational setting, contextualisation involves reaffirming traditional beliefs while continuously adapting their expression to environmental conditions. Uncovering and committing to the enduring aspects of ideology in the Christian organisational management discourse is a great consideration for Christian strategic managers as they apply strategic management concepts. Although much can be learned from strategic managers in the business world about market analysis, competitive strategy, comparative advantages, marketing and customer service, it is wise to take the underlying philosophy with a grain of salt; nonprofit organisations are not businesses and strategic leaders and managers of profit and nonprofit organisations play different roles.[77] The later operates under tighter constraints than their private sector counterparts in three important areas, namely, defining the mission, objectives, and the strategy of their organisations; designing and managing internal operations and interacting with external constituencies. The differences between public, nonprofit and for-profit organisations include environmental factors, transactional processes, and organisational characteristics.[78] The flexibility of public and nonprofit organisations to respond to market shifts is severely constrained by a web of inter-organisational contracts, legal mandates, negotiated franchises, limited control over diverse stakeholders, and political pressures from all sides.

It is not accurate to suggest that nonprofit executives can fully embrace the business frame of mind toward strategic management as their role in society is qualitatively different. [79] There are important philosophical differences to keep in mind; the mission must follow the mandate; to think of citizens only as customers is to degrade their role in society; an organisations portfolio will always have loss leaders and managing external constituencies is essential to organisational success. Even though they ultimately answer to shareholders and directors, business executives can define, refine, and redefine the mission and corporate strategy of their organisations with relative ease. Their mandate, which they receive from shareholders through the board of directors, and their mission are essentially indistinguishable.

Nonprofit executives, however, must strike a more reflective and sometimes delicate balance between mandate and mission. For the most part, business executives are rewarded for simply delivering a valued product at a fair price. They are held responsible and accountable to their shareholders for delivering a quality product and producing a profit for the company. However, nonprofit managers are stewards of the public trust and enforcers of societal values. As stewards, they must be more deliberative and inclusive in their decision making than entrepreneurs, who need to act quickly to take advantage of market shifts. Business executives, knowing that their primary objective is to make a profit and increase shareholder value, can abandon losing products and services very quickly. In nonprofit organisations, an executive's primary objective is to serve people, regardless of financial performance. Making a profit on certain services may help an executive accomplish that goal, but profit making is incidental to the primary mission of filling social needs that are not filled by the private market. Hence, the strategic manager's approach to portfolio management will, by definition, be much different from that of the typical business executive and the approach to portfolio design will be focused primarily on mission fulfilment.[80]

The ideological nature of strategy and the need to keep philosophical differences between profit and nonprofit organisations in mind means that Christian social enterprise organisations should have an approach to strategic management that, while borrowing from the most helpful and relevant business ideas, allows the nonprofit organisation to achieve success without compromising its unique mission, constituency and core Christian values. In this regard the concepts and tools of strategy analysis, based on ideologies that formed the backbone of the strategy literature, need a basic re-evaluation in order to pave the way for new ideas that accommodate nonprofit Christian organisations.

Strategizing

Implicit in the ideological underpinnings of the concepts and tools in the strategy field is the need for an approach to strategy that takes on board the unique purpose and characteristics of the Christian social enterprise organisation. Despite all the signpost for rethinking strategy, there exists an academic disillusionment in some quarters and some managers engage in strategic experiments without guidance of appropriate theories.[81] The perspectives on strategic thinking, the purpose of the organisation and the use of strategy show that strategy as practiced by Christian strategic managers is potentially different from strategy in other contexts.

> *The philosophical differences between profit and nonprofit organisations mean that Christian social enterprise organisations should have an approach to strategic management that, while borrowing from the most helpful and relevant business ideas, allows them to achieve success without compromising their unique mission, constituency and core values.*

The term strategizing has been used by some writers in the strategy field to refer to the 'doing of strategy' and it is the focal point of the 'strategy-as-practice' school of thought.[82] This view is concerned with how individual managers do strategy, on a day-to-day basis and the 'situated, concrete activity' in which they partake. [83] Strategic management, in the Christian organisational context, incorporates intuition and spiritual sensitivity in strategy development. The practice of strategy in this context means that social enterprise Christian strategic managers cannot fully embrace the business frame of mind toward strategic management as their role in society is qualitatively different.

Strategizing is 'doing strategy' in context; a context that influences the strategic process and strategy content. The strategy-as-practice view builds upon and complements research into strategy process which looks at the actions that lead and support strategy [84] and how is and should, strategy be made, analysed, dreamt-up, formulated, implemented, changed and controlled.[85] Christian managers used both formal and informal planning processes. Although the traditional view of the strategic process is one of a structured, planned, rational process, the role of the non-rational, informal, more social processes is essential.[86] Strategy is looked at as a verb, to strategize, with an emphasis on the doing of strategy, rather than as a noun, looking at strategy or strategies (the focus of strategy content research); to understand strategizing better, there is the need to closely observe strategists as they work their way through their strategy making routines.[87]

The concept of strategizing in the strategic management field opens up avenues to explore strategy practice in the Christian social enterprise context. Depending on the assumptions, strategizing, using a variety of theoretical approaches can be looked at as facts, as sense making or as discourse.

Notes

[1] Richard Lynch. *Corporate Strategy* (Harlow: FT Prentice Hall, 2006), 651

[2] See E. Vaara. 'On the discursive construction of success/failure in narratives of postmerger integration ' *Organisation Studies*, 23,2002: 211-248.

[3] See Gary Hamel and, C. K. Prahalad. 'Strategic intent.' *Harvard Business Review*, May-June, 1989: 63-76.

[4] B. Lovas and S. Ghoshal. 'Strategy as guided evolution.' *Strategic Management Journal*, 21, 2000: 885.

[5] See R.R. Nelson and S.G. Winter. *An Evolutionary Theory of Economic Change.* (Cambridge, MA: BelKnap Press of Harvard University, 1982), 99-107.

[6] See J.R. Searle, *The construction of social reality.* (Free Press: New York, 995),9.

[7] See Gary Hamel and, C. K. Prahalad. 'Strategic intent.' *Harvard Business Review*, May-June, 1989: 63-76.

[3] Peter M. Senge. *The fifth discipline:the art and practice of the learning organisation.* (New York:Doubleday/Currency, 1990),20.

[9] See Gary Hamel and, C. K. Prahalad. 'Strategic intent.' *Harvard Business Review*, May-June, 1989: 63-76.

[10] See Richard Scott. *Institutions and organisations.* (London:Sage, 1995),

[11] Gerry Johnson and Kevin Scholes, *Exploring Corporate Strategy* (London: FT Prentice Hall, 1999), 60.

[12] Rodney Stark and William Bainbridge, *A Theory of Religion.* (New York: Peter Lang, 1987),42.

[13] Richard Lynch. *Corporate Strategy* (Harlow: FT Prentice Hall, 2006), 342-343.

[14] Austin, James, Stevenson, H. and J.Wei-Skillern. 'Social and Commercial Entrepreneurship: Same, Different. or Both?" *Entrepreneurship Theory and Practice*, 30, 2006:1.

[15] Peter Brierley. *Coming up Trumps. Four Ways into the Future* (Milton Keynes : Authentic Media, 2004), 174.

[16] Peter Brierley. *Coming up Trumps. Four Ways into the Future* (Milton Keynes : Authentic Media, 2004), 174.

[17] Tom Copeland, Tim Koller and Jack Murrin (McKinsey and Company , Inc.) *Valuation: Measuring the Value of Companies* (New York:John Wiley, 2000), 45.

[18] See for example M. Granovetter. "Economic action and social structure: the problem of embeddedness."*American Journal of Sociology* 91, 1985: 481-510.

[19] See AS Huff. *Mapping Strategic Thought* (Chichester: John Wiley & Son,1990),21

[20] Paul R. Nevin. *Balanced Scorecard Step by Step* (New York:John Wiley & Sons, Inc., 2002), 22.

[21] Paul R. Nevin. 35.

[22] Robert S. Kaplan and David P. Norton, "The Balanced Scorecard: Measures that drive performance." *Harvard Business Review*, January-February 1992, 71-79.

[23] Robert S. Kaplan and David P. Norton. *The Strategy-Focused Organisation:How Balanced Scorecard Companies Thrive in the New Business Environment.* (Massachusetts: Harvard Business Press, 2001), 134.

[24] Paul R. Nevin. *Balanced Scorecard Step by Step* (New York:John Wiley & Sons, Inc., 2002), 36.

[25] Richard Lynch. *Corporate Strategy* (Harlow: FT Prentice Hall, 2006),345.

[26] See for instance Y. Boshyk, 'Beyond knowledge management'. *Financial Times Mastering Information Management*, 8 Feb, pp12-13.

[27] Austin, James, Stevenson, H. and J.Wei-Skillern. 'Social and Commercial Entrepreneurship: Same, Different, or Both?" *Entrepreneurship Theory and Practice*, 30, 2006:1

[28] See R.M. Kanter and D. Summers. "Doing well while doing good: Dilemmas of performance measurement in nonprofit organisations and the need for a multiple-constituency approach", in *The nonprofit sector: A research handbook*).ed. W.W. Powell (New Haven: Yale University Press,1987), 156.

[29] Ken Starkey and Sue Tempest. "Bowling along: strategic management and social Capital." *European management review*, 1, 2004:80.

[30] Jane Kay. The stakeholder corporation, in G.Kelly, D. Kelly and A. Gamble (eds).*Stakeholder Captialism.* (Basingstoke: McMillan, 1997),

[31] Ken Starkey and Sue Tempest. "Bowling along: strategic management and social Capital." *European management review*, 1, 2004:80

[32] See W. Hutton, "An overview of stakeholding, in G.Kelly, D.Kelly and A.Gamble (eds.) *Stakeholder capitalism.*(Basingstoke:Macmillan,1997).

[33] Gerry Johnson and Kevin Scholes, *Exploring Corporate Strategy* (London: FT Prentice Hall, 1999),213.

[34] Claire Capon. *Understanding Organisational Context.*(Harlow: Pearson Education, 2000),333.

[35] See Jeanne M. Liedka. Linking strategic thinking with strategic planning. *Strategy and Leadership*, October, 1, 1998:120-129.

[36] John Adair. Strategic Leadership

[37] Peter Brierley, 173

[38] Gary Hamel and Prahalad, strategic intent. Harvard Business Review. 63-76.

[39] Ian Wilson 1994.

[40] Henry Mintzberg, 1994. The rise and fall of strategic planning

[41] See for example Ralph Stacey, 1992. *Managing the Unknowable.* Jossey Bass: San Francisco.

[42] See Jeanne M. Liedka."Strategic thinking; can it be taught?, *Long Range Planning*, 31, 1998:120-129.

[43] Peter Senge 1990. The fifth discipline: the art and practice of the learning organisation. (New York:Double day/Currency:1990),

[44] See Jeanne M. Liedka. Linking strategic thinking with strategic planning. *Strategy and Leadership*, October, 1, 1998:120-129.

[45] Peter Brierley, *Leadership, Vision and Growing Churches.* (London: Christian Research, 2003),3.

[46] John Adair. Strategic Leadership

[47] See L. Heracleous. "Strategic thinking or strategic planning." *Long RangePlanning*, 31, 1998:481-487

[48] See Jeanne M. Liedka. Linking strategic thinking with strategic planning.

[49] Tony Grundy and Laura Brown, *Be Your Own Strategy Consultant: Demystifying Strategic Thinking* (London: Thomson Learning,2002), 226.

[50] See Jeanne M. Liedka. Linking strategic thinking with strategic planning.

[51] See Jeanne M. Liedka. Linking strategic thinking with strategic planning.

[52] Peter Brierley, *Coming up Trumps. Four Ways into the Future* (Milton Keynes : Authentic Media, 2004), ix.

[53] Gerry Johnson and Kevin Scholes, 26.

[54] Henry Mintzberg. 'Crafting Strategy'. *Harvard Business Review*, 65,1987:66 75.

[55] Gerry Johnson and Kevin Scholes, 26.

[56] See Ralph Stacey, 'Strategy as order emerging from chaos'. *Long Range Planning*, 26,1993:10-13.

[57] Gerry Johnson and Kevin Scholes, 26.

[58] Gerry Johnson and Kevin Scholes, 34.

[59] Timothy Robnett and Allen H.Quist. *The Spirit Driven Church.* (Colorado Springs:Victor, 2006), 210.

[60] Paul Shrivastava. Is strategic management ideological? *Journal of Management* 12(3), 1986, :364.

[61] Paul Shrivastava. Is strategic management ideological? *Journal of Management* 12(3), 1986, :364.

[62] See for instance M. Billig, *Ideology and Opinions.* (London: Sage, 1991),15.

[63] See M. Knights and G. Morgan. "Corporate strategy, organisations and subjectivity: a critique. *Organisational Studies*, 12, 1991:251-273

[64] Timothy Robnett and Allen H.Quist. *The Spirit Driven Church.* (Colorado Springs:Victor, 2006),162.

[65] Mahmoud Ezzamel and Hugh Willmott. "Rethinking strategy: contemporary perspectives and debates." *European Management Review*, 1, 2004:47.

[66] David Knights and G. Morgan. "Corporate strategy, organisations and subjectivity: a critique. *Organisational Studies*, 12, 1991:252.

[67] David Knights and G. Morgan.

[68] See N. Fairclough, N *Discourse and Social Change.* {Cambridge: Polity,

1992).71

[69] See D. Barry and M. Elmes. "Strategy retold: toward a narrative view of strategy discourse.*Academy of Management Review*, 22, 1997:430

[70] David Knights and G. Morgan,252

[71] Pete Thomas. Ideology and the Discourse of Strategic Management: A Critical Research Framework

[72] Toby Hardy. http://www. mngt.waikato.ac.nz/ejrot/Vol4_1/harfield.pdf

[73] See for example David Knights, "Changing spaces: the disruptive impact of a new epistemological location for the study of management." *Academy of Management Review* 17, 1992:514-36.

[74] David Knights, 514-36.

[75] Toby Hardy. http://www. mngt.waikato.ac.nz/ejrot/Vol4_1/harfield.pdf

[76] See Richard Whittington, *What is Strategy and Does It Matter?* (London: Routledge, 1993),56

[77] Kevin P. Kearns, *Private Sector Strategies for Social Sector Success: the guide to strategy and planning for public and nonprofit organisations* (San Francisco: Jossey-Bass Inc., 2000), 27

[78] See Paul C Nutt and Robert W. Backoff. "Organisational publicness and its implications for strategic management". *Journal of Public Administration Research and Theory* , 3, 1993:209-231.

[79] Kevin P. Kearns, 29.

[80] Kevin P. Kearns, 29.

[81] Henk W. Vorbeda, "Crisis in Strategy," *European Management Review* 1, 2000: 35.

[82] Richard Whittington. "Strategy as practice". *Long Range Planning.* 29, 1996:731

[83] See for example Richard Whittington. "The work of strategizing and organising: for a practice perspective." *Strategic organisation*, 1, 2003:119-127

[84] See for example A.S Huff and R.K Reger. "A review of strategic process research." *Journal of Management*, 13, 1987: 212

[85] See for example B. DeWit and R. Meyer. *Strategy process, content, context: An international perspective.* (London: Thomas Learning, 2004), 5.

[86] See A. Bailey, G. Johnson and K. Daniels. "Validation of a multi-dimensional measure of strategy development processes". *British Journal of Management*, 11, 2000: 152.

[87]Richard Whittington. "Strategy as practice". *Long Range Planning.* 29, 1996:731

6

FORWARD LOOKING STRATEGY

Strategic management is increasingly being conceptualised. It is important that theory development and practice are informed by the practices and norms in different contexts, such as the Christian social enterprise organisation. It is also important for the forward looking strategic management field, not only to understand how strategic management shapes the organisation but also how the unique purpose of the organisation itself shapes strategic management.

It is clear that the effective leadership and management of organizations require good strategic thinking and management. It is not surprising that social sector organisations use private sector strategic management methods. However, the strategic context of the social organisation is broader than its business counterpart and that of religious organisations is additionally complex as they are social enterprises that create, maintain, and exchange supernatural compensators bundled with rewards.

> *It is important for the forward looking strategy field, not only to understand how strategic management shapes the organisation but also how the unique purpose of the organisation itself shapes strategic management.*

Perspectives on organisational purpose show its role in shaping strategic purpose and intent, value creation and strategizing. Christian social enterprises exist to deliver 'spiritual value' and social value. The overriding purpose of the organisation is the guiding principle for its strategic intent, providing the sense of direction and destiny for all the stakeholders of the organisation. Thus, the ultimate purpose for the use of strategy is to deliver the same ends of spiritual and social values. Strategy is a means to an end. Economic value is both incidental and subservient, from a balanced scorecard perspective, to achieving 'socio-spiritual' value.

The purpose of the organisation also shapes the ultimate purpose and content of strategy development. The stakeholder perspective is more appropriate for social enterprises as in this case, the organisation is viewed as joint venture between a number of its participants, each of whom has a stake in the purpose of the organisation. That God is a stakeholder with controlling interest means that biblical perspectives on His Word and Will shape the ultimate purpose of the organisation.

It is suggested that for nonprofits to transform lofty aspirations into quantifiable impact, they need to become more familiar with traditional business tools. Such tools must be adapted to espoused purposes. In as much as strategic thinking adds diverse value, the high-level purpose of the organisation itself determines how value is prioritised. The concept of 'contextual value added', therefore, acknowledges the importance of value creation but also recognises that value and its measure, must be qualified to be meaningful and helpful for social enterprise managers.

Strategic thinking and strategic planning work in tandem within the same strategic management framework. Managers apply strategic thinking both through formal and informal planning processes; intuition and 'spiritual' sensitivity are part of the informal process. Getting more value from the use of strategic thinking includes tailoring key concepts to the unique circumstances of the organisation. The values, expectations and ideologies of different stakeholders play important roles in the development of strategy, and this is particularly the case where the purpose of the organisation is rooted in such values. The purpose of the Christian organisation is rooted in its spiritual values and theology. Fundamental to strategizing, that is 'doing' strategy, is the context and the Christian strategic managers' philosophy and frame of mind toward strategic management. Social sector Christian strategic managers cannot embrace fully the business frame of mind toward strategic management as their role in society is qualitatively different and there are important philosophical differences to keep in mind.

Further elaboration

The distinctive purpose of the Christian social enterprise organisation influences the use of strategy by creating value and conceptions different from those of business organisations. This provides opportunities for further elaboration by strategic management researchers and practitioners on effective approaches to social enterprise strategic management in the religious domain.

What are the relevant strategy concepts and tools developed for business organisations that the Christian strategic manager may borrow without undermining espoused purposes and philosophy? There is need to understand from a comparative analysis approach, the extent to which elements applicable to strategic management in business organisations, that have been more extensively studied, are transferable to religious social enterprise strategic management. Such studies would further identify common and differentiating features between business and social enterprise strategic management. To some extent, it should also provide information on the ways in which insights from Christian social enterprise strategic management can contribute to a deeper understanding of traditional business strategic management.

> *The distinctive purpose of the Christian social enterprise organisation influences the use of strategy by creating value and conceptions different from those of business organisations*

'Spiritual value', is a useful Christian managerial metaphor to explore new aspects of strategic management, especially areas of organisational life that are intangible. Additionally, the strategic management field has been enriched by different schools of thought and ideologies and might benefit from a systematic christian theological viewpoint. In this direction, understanding the process of strategizing by Christian strategic managers, particularly on the use of both informal (intuitive/ spiritual insights) and formal planning processes to craft and implement strategy, may inform the nature of strategic leadership and decision making. If strategy is to be understood as what an organisation's strategic managers do daily, and not what is captured with strategic plan documents that are opened once in a while, then a broader understanding of strategizing and strategic managing offers value.

Bibliography

Ahenkora, K and Peasah, O. Crafting strategy that measures up. *International Journal of Business and Management* 6, 2011:278-283.

Andrews, K.R. *The Concept of Corporate Strategy*. Homewood II: Dow Jones-Irwin, 1971.

Argyris, Chris. "Teaching smart people how to learn". *Harvard Business Review*,(May-June, 1991): 99.

Austin, James, Stevenson, H. and J.Wei-Skillern. 'Social and Commercial Entrepreneurship: Same, Different, or Both?" *Entrepreneurship Theory and Practice*, 30, 2006:1-12. http://dx.coi.org/10.1111/j.1540-6520.2006.00107.x

Bailey, A., G. Johnson and K. Daniels. "Validation of a multi-dimensional measure of strategy development processes". *British Journal of Management*, 11, 2000: 152-162. http://dx.doi.org/10.1111/1467-8551.t01-1-00157

Barry, B. and M. Elmes. "Strategy retold: toward a narrative view of strategy discourse. *Academy of Management Review*, 22, 1997:429-452.

Berger, Peter L. *The Sacred Canopy*. New York: Doubleday, 1967.

Bettis, Richard and M.A.Hitt "The New Competitive Landscape", *Strategic Management Journal*, 16, 1995:7-19. http://dx.doi.org/10.1002/smj.4250160915

Billig, M. *Ideology and Opinions*. (London: Sage, 1991), 5-20.

Bosch, David J. *Transforming Mission: Paradigm Shifts in Theology of Mission*. Maryknoll, NY:Orbis Books, 1991.

Boshyk, Y. 'Beyond knowledge management'. *Financial Times Mastering Information Management*, 8 Feb, pp12-13.

Brierley, Peter. *Coming up Trumps. Four Ways into the Future*.Milton Keynes : Authentic Media, 2004.

Brierley, Peter. *Leadership, Vision and Growing Churches*. London :Christian Research, 2003.

Brierley, Peter. *The tide is running out*. London :Christian Research, 2000.

Chander, Alfred. *Strategy and Structure*. Cambridge, Mass: MIT Press, 1962.

Camera, C. "Redirecting research in business policy and strategy." *Strategic Management Journal*, 6, 1985:1-15. http://dx.doi.org/10.1002/smj.4250060102

Capon, Claire . *Understanding Organisational Context.* Harlow: Pearson Education, 2000.

Chavez, M. "Denominations as dual structures: an organisational analysis." *Sociology of Religion,* 54,1993:147-169. http://dx.doi.org/10.2307/3712137

Copeland, Tom, Tim Koller and Jack Murrin (McKinsey and Company, Inc) *Valuation: Measuring the Value of Companies.* New York: John Wiley, 2000.

De Kare Silver, Michael *Strategy in Crisis* (Basingstoke: Macmillan Press,1997.

DeWit, B. and R. Meyer. *Strategy: Process, Content, Context: An International Perspective.* London: Thomson Learning, 2004.

Drucker, Peter F. *Managing the nonprofit organisation.*New York: HarperCollins Publishers,1992.

Drucker, Peter F. *Practice of Management.* London: Mercury, 1961.

Ezzamel, Mahmoud and Hugh Willmott. "Rethinking strategy: contemporary perspectives and debates." *European Management Review,* 1, 2004:43-48.

Fahey, Laim and Robert M. Randall. "Managing Marketplace Strategy." In *The Portable MBA in Strategy,* eds. Liam Fahey and Robert M. Randall, 8.New York: John Wiley & Sons, 2001.

Fairclough, N. *Discourse and Social Change.* {Cambridge: Polity, 2002).

Fifield, Paul. *Marketing Strategy.* London: Butterworth-Heinmann, 1998.

Finke, Roger. "The consequences of competition: supply-side explanations for religious change." In *Rational Choice Theory and Religion: Summary and Assessment,* ed. Young, L.A., 45-64. New York:Routledge Presss, 1997..

Finke, Roger and R. Stark, *The Churching of America, 1776-1990:Winners and Losers in Our Religious Economy* (New Brunswick: Rutgers University Press, 1992),21.

Giligan, Colin and R.M.S. Wilson, *Strategic Marketing Planning.*London: Butterworth Heinemann, 2003.

Gills, Robert. *A Vision for Growth.* London: SPCK, 1994.

Granovetter, M. "Economic action and social structure: the problem of embeddedness." *American Journal of Sociology* 91, 1985: 481-510.

Grundy, Tony and Laura Brown. *Be Your Own Strategy Consultant: Demystifying Strategic Thinking.* London: Thomson Learning, 2002.

Hamel, Gary. *Leading the revolution.*Boston, MA: Harvard Business School Press, 2000.

Hamel, Gary and C. K. Prahalad. 'Strategic intent.' *Harvard Business Review,*

May-June, 1989: 63-76.

Hardy, Toby. http://www. mngt.waikato.ac.nz/ejrot/Vol4_1/harfield.htm accessed 2nd March 2007

Heracleous, L. "Strategic thinking or strategic planning." *Long RangePlanning,*

31, 1998:481-487
http://www.valuebasedmanagement.net/faq_shareholder_stakeholder_per
spective.htm accessed 27th June 2006.
http:// .valuebasedmanagement.net/faq_history_value_based_
management.html. accessed 27th June 2006.
http://www.valuebasedmanagement.net, accessed 27th June 2006.

Huff, AS. *Mapping Strategic Thought,* Chichester: John Wiley & Son,1990.
Huff, AS. & R.K, Reger."A review of strategic process research". *Journal of
Management.* 13, 1987:217-236.

Hutton, W. "An overview of stakeholding, in G.Kelly, D.Kelly and
A.Gamble (eds.) *Stakeholder capitalism.*(Basingstoke:Macmillan,1997).
Iannaccone, Lawrence R.1995. "Risk, rationality and religious portfolios."
Economic   Inquiry,   33:   285-289.   http://dx.doi.org/10.1111/j.1465-
7295.1995.tb01863.x
Johnson, Gerry and Kevin, Scholes. *Exploring Corporate Strategy.*London: FT
Prentice Hall, 1999.

Kanter, R.M. and D. Summers. "Doing well while doing good: Dilemmas
of performance measurement in nonprofit organisations and the need
for a multiple-constituency approach", in *The nonprofit sector: A research
handbook).ed.* W.W. Powell (New Haven: Yale University Press,1987),
154-166.

Kaplan, Robert S. and David P. Norton, "The Balanced Scorecard:
Measures that drive performance." *Harvard Business Review*, January-
February 1992, 71-79.
Kay, Jane. "The stakeholder corporation." In *Stakeholder Captialism* .
eds.G.Kelly, D. Kelly and A. Gamble. Basingstoke: McMillan, 1997.
Kay, John. *Foundations of Corporate Success*, Oxford:Oxford University Press,
1993.

Kearns, Kevin P. *Private Sector Strategies for Social Sector Success: the guide to
strategy and planning for public and nonprofit organisations.* San Francisco:
Jossey-Bass Inc., 2000.
Knights, David (1992) "Changing spaces: the disruptive impact of a new
epistemological location for the study of management." *Academy of
Management Review* 17, 1992:514-36.

Knights, David and G. Morgan. "Corporate strategy, organisations and
subjectivity: a   critique. *Organisational   Studies,*   12,   1991:251-273.
http://dx.doi.org/10.1177/017084069101200205

Koch, Robert. *The Financial Times guide to Strategy: how to create and deliver a
useful strategy.* London: Prentice Hall, 2000.

Leedy, Paul D. and Jeanne. E. Omrod, *Practical Research: Planning and Design,*

6th ed..Upper Saddle River,NJ:Prentice-Hall, Inc.,1997.

Levitt, Theodore. "Marketing Myopia", *Harvard Business Review*, 38 (4), 1960: 45-56

Liedka, Jeanne M. "Strategic thinking; can it be taught?", *Long Range Planning*, 31, 1998:120-129. http://dx.doi.org/10.1016/S0024-6301(97)00098-8

Liedka, Jeanne M. "Linking strategic thinking with strategic planning", *Strategy and Leadership*, October, 1, 1998:120-129.

Lovas, B. and S. Ghoshal. "Strategy as guided evolution", *Strategic Management Journal*, 21, 2000: 875-896. http://dx.doi.org/10.1002/1097-0266(200009)21:9<875::AID-SMJ126>3.0.CO;2-P

Lynch, Richard. *Corporate Strategy*. Harlow: FT Prentice Hall, 2006.

Mahoney, T.J. "Strategic management and determinism: sustaining the conversation." *Journal of Management Studies*, 30, 1993:173-191. http://dx.doi.org/10.1111/j.1467-6486.1993.tb00300.x

Miller, Kent D. "Competitive Strategies of Religious Organisations." *Strategic Management Journal* 23, 2002:435-456.

Mintzberg, Henry. "The Fall and Rise of Strategic planning." *Harvard Business Review*, 1993:107-114.

Mintzberg , Henry. *The Rise and Fall of Strategic planning*. New York:Simon and Schuster Inc., 1993.

Mintzberg, Henry and J.A. Walters. "Of strategies, deliberate and emergent." *Strategic Management Journal*, 6, 2003:257-272

Mintzberg, Henry . "The Design School: reconsidering the basic premises of strategic Management." *Strategic Management Journal*, 11,1990:176-95.

Nelson, R.R. and S.G. Winter. *An Evolutionary Theory of Economic Change*. (Cambridge, MA: BelKnap Press of Harvard University, 1982).

Nevin, Paul R.. *Balanced Scorecard Step by Step* (New York:John Wiley & Sons, Inc., 2002), 22.

Nutt, Paul C and Robert W. Backoff. "Organisational publicness and its implications for strategic management". *Journal of Public Administration Research and Theory* , 3, 1993:209-231.

Prahalad, C.K. and Richard Bettis. "The dominant logic: new linkage between diversity and performance." *Strategic Management Journal*, 7, 1986:485-501.

Prahalad ,C.K. and Gary Hamel, "The Core Competence of the Corporation." *Harvard Business Review*, 1990:79-91.

Prahalad, C.K. and Gary Hamel. "Strategy as a field of study: why search for a new paradigm?" *Strategic Management Journal*, 15, 1994:5-16

Pettigrew , Andrew. *The Awakening Giant: Continuity and Change at ICI*. Oxford: Blackwell,1985.

Porter, Michael E. "The State of Strategic Thinking." *The Economist* , May 23,1987

Porter, Michael E. "Toward a dynamic theory of strategy." *Strategic Management Journal*, 12:1991:95-117.

Porter, Michael E. *Competitive Advantage: Creating and Sustaining Superior Performance.* New York: Free Press, 1985.

Porter, Michael E. "How competitive forces shape strategy." *Harvard Business Review*, 57, 1979:37-145.

Quinn, J.B. "Managing strategic change." *Sloan Management Review*, 21, 1980:3-20.

Robnett, Timothy and Allen H.Quist. *The Spirit Driven Church.* (Colorado Springs:Victor, 2006).

Roller, R.H , "Strategy Formulation in Nonprofit Social Services Organisations: A proposed framework." *Nonprofit management and leadership*, 7, 1996:137-153

Sampler, Jeffrey L. "Digital Strategy." In *The Portable MBA in Strategy.*eds. Laim Fahey and R. M. Randall, 132 New York: John Wiley & Sons, 2001.

Searle, J.R. *The construction of social reality.* (Free Press: New York, 1995).

Senge, Peter M. "The leaders new work: building learning organisations." *Sloan Management Review*, 1990: 7-22.

Senge, Peter M. *The fifth discipline:the art and practice of the learning organisation.* (New York:Doubleday/Currency, 1990).

Sentence, Andrew. *Successful Leadership in a Competitive Environment.* London: Christian Research,2003.

Shrivastava, Paul. Is strategic management ideological? *Journal of Management* 12(3), 1986:363-377. http://dx.doi.org/10.1177/014920638601200305

Skloot, E., ed. *The nonprofit entrepreneur: creating ventures to earn income.* New York: Foundation Center, 1988.

Stark , Rodney and William Bainbridge, *A Theory of Religion.* New York: Peter Lang, 1987.

Starkey, Ken and Sue Tempest. "Bowling along: strategic management and social capital." *European management review*, 1, 2004: 78-83. http://dx.doi.org/10.1057/palgrave.emr.1500007

Sunderland, Jonathan and Canwell, Dianne. *Key Concepts in Strategic Management.* Basingstoke : Palgrave Mcmillan, 2004.

Teece, D.J. "Contributions and impediments of economic analysis to the study of strategic management." In *Perspectives on strategic management*, ed. J.W. Fredrickson, New York: Harper and Row, 1990.

Teece, David J., Pisano Gary. and Amy Shuen, "Dynamic capabilities and strategic management. *Strategic Management Journal,*Vol 18:7, 509-533. http://dx.doi.org/10.1002/(SICI)1097-0266(199708)18:7<509::AID-SMJ882>3.0.CO;2-Z

Thompson, Arthur A., and A.J. (Lonnie) Strickland, *Crafting and Executing*

Strategy. New York: McGraw-Hill, 2001.

Thompson, John L. *Strategy in Action.* London: International Thompson Business Press, 1995.

Tzu, Sun. *The Art of War.* New York: Harper Collins,1994.

Vorbeda, Henk, W. "Crisis in Strategy." *European Management Review* 1, 2000:35-42. Whittington, Richard. *What is strategy-and does it matter?* London: Routledge,1993. http://dx.doi.org/10.1016/0024-6301(96)00068-4

Whittington, Richard. "Strategy as practice". *Long Range Planning* 29,1996:731-735.

Whittington, Richard. "The work of strategizing and organising: for a practice perspective." *Strategic organisation*, 1, 2003:119-127.

Whittington, Richard. A. Pettigrew and H.Thomas. eds. *Handbook of Strategy and Management.* London: Sage, 2002.

Wilson, Ian. "There is no Universal Strategy Formula." In *The Portable MBA in Strategy*, eds. Laim Fahey and Robert M. Randall, 385. New York: John Wiley & Sons. 2001.

Zaleski ,P. and C. Zech. "The optimal size of a religious congregation: and economic theory of clubs analysis. *American Journal of Economics and Sociology*,54:1995:439-453.http://dx.doi.org/10.1111/j.1536-7150.1995.tb03249.x

www.ingramcontent.com/pod-product-compliance
Lightning Source LLC
Chambersburg PA
CBHW060359050426
42449CB00009B/1809